# POLITICAL ISSUES MADE EASY

# POLITICAL ISSUES MADE EASY

A Made *Easy* Series Book

Kenneth L. Gentry, Jr., Th.D.

VICTORIOUS HOPE
PUBLISHING

Chesnee, South Carolina 29323
"Proclaiming the kingdom of God and teaching those things which
concern the Lord Jesus Christ, with all confidence."
(Acts 28:31)

Published by:
Victorious Hope Publishing
P.O. Box 285
Chesnee, South Carolina 29323

Website: www.VictoriousHope.com

*Printed in the United States of America*

Cover design by Brian Godawa

ISBN 978-0-9964525-8-8

**Victorious Hope Publishing** is committed to producing Christian educational materials for promoting the whole Bible for the whole of life. We are conservative, evangelical, and Reformed and are committed to the doctrinal formulation found in the Westminster Standards.

# IN MEMORY OF

## Ramon Arias

Faithful Servant of Christ
Biblical Worldview Advocate
Christian Patriot

# TABLE OF CONTENTS

# PREFACE

Beginning with the Presidency of Barack Hussein Obama (2008–2015), America began a radical shift to the left. In doing so, the nation was leaving behind its Christian foundations, Constitutional moorings, and common sense.

It is unfortunate that many evangelical Christians are alarmed at the direction the country is taking. This is unfortunate because they *all* should be. Christians *must* understand the issues and take a stand against this leftward lurch. We must do so if we are to have any hope for America continuing as it was originally founded — as a Constitutional Republic.

This book was originally published in 2012 under the title *Political Christianity*. It was published with a pseudonym ("Christian Citizen"); I was the "Christian Citizen" who wrote it. The only part of the original that I did not write was the Appendix. The publisher edited it by taking my final chapter and adding a alternative position in order to provide "balance." That Appendix has now been removed, returned to its original form, and re-inserted as the final chapter. This chapter is my argument in defense of voting for the lesser-of-evils (see ch. 8 below).

Much has changed dramatically in these last few years. Consequently, some of the negative alarms sounded within have actually come-to-pass. Though slightly dated now, most of these have been retained in the current edition. This is in order to demonstrate from where we have come and to show how we have gotten to this point. Maintaining much of the concerns as originally expressed in the 2012 edition will show the reality and danger of slippery-slope concerns.

Christian apologist Cornelius Van Til warned of the deleterious effect of unbelief. He warned of a society's "integration downward into the void" when it turns from Christian truth and begins to "suppress the truth in unrighteousness" (Rom. 1:18). I hope this book will motivate Christians to get involved in social and political discourse with a view to reversing our dangerous downward slide.

Actually, we are no longer caught in a downward *slide*. Rather, we are now witnessing a full-scale *collapse* of our society, culture, and legal system. We must apply Paul's concerned observation and committed determination:

"The weapons of our warfare are not of the flesh, but divinely powerful for the destruction of fortresses. We are destroying speculations and every lofty thing raised up against the knowledge of God, and we are taking every thought captive to the obedience of Christ." (2 Cor. 10:4–5)

Come, let us reason together!

# INTRODUCTION

Modern social etiquette holds that it is not polite to talk about either religion or politics. In this book I will be writing about both religion and politics. So in order to be polite, please do not read it aloud.

Despite the modern conventions of social etiquette, however, we are Christians and cannot avoid talking about our faith. And because politics impacts our daily lives, we should discuss and understand politics. And because of this we simply *must* talk about religion and politics.

## Our Sad Situation

One of the main reasons for the fear of political discussions is the sad state of political affairs today. A satirical dictionary on politics is so close to the truth that we do not know whether to laugh or to cry. The dictionary entry for the word "politics" itself is defined as:

> "Politics. 1. a strife of interests masquerading as a contest of principles. 2. The conduct of public affairs for private advantage. 3. The skilled use of blunt objects."

Indeed, this dictionary's defines "bad government" as "the result of letting politicians win elections."

Some would say that such humorous definitions as just presented arise from the sad fact that 90% of the politicians give the other 10% a bad name. Yet, rather than discouraging Christians from speaking of or engaging in politics, this should really exercise the opposite effect. *Because of* these problems the political world absolutely *needs* a Christian influence. And that is what this book encourages.

Not only so but we must consider:

## Our God's Revelation

Early in the Bible God establishes a people for himself, a "kingdom of priests" that was to function as a "holy nation" (Exo. 19:6). To Israel he gave laws to govern them as a nation, as a civil-body politic: "Now, O Israel, listen to the statutes and the judgments which I am teaching you to perform, so that you may live and go in and take possession of the land which the LORD, the God of your fathers, is giving you" (Deut. 4:1).

When we open the Bible we find God's law designed for a nation in its foundational books (particularly Exodus and Deuteronomy). Not only so, but we also hear God spoken of as a king (Psa. 5:2; 44:4; 47:6–7; 68:24; 84:3; 145:1; Isa. 43:15; 44:6). We read of God's prophets often either speaking about or directly confronting kings of both Israel (Isa. 37:10; 39:3; Jer. 17:20; 19:3; 22:8) and the nations (Isa. 14:4; 39:3; 45:1; Jer. 46:25; Eze. 29:3; 31:2; 32:2).

When we come to the New Testament we discover political concerns continuing. The language of God's dealings with his people continues to reflect political realities, for God's saving work in the world is called a "kingdom." Consequently, the "kingdom of God" (or of heaven) is an important topic in the preaching of Jesus (Matt. 12:28; 19:24; 21:31; Mark 1:15; 4:11ff; John 3:3, 5), Paul (Acts 28:23; Rom. 14:17; 1 Cor. 6:9), and others (Heb. 12:28; 2 Pet. 1:11; Rev 1:6, 9; 5:10; 11:15). In Romans 13 Paul establishes clear principles that must govern the Christian's outlook on government. Peter does the same in 1 Peter 2.

Thus, not only does our political mess today obligate us to be more political, but when we look at the Bible we see a document that is largely political itself. What are we to do? How are we to become politically engaged *as Christians*?

## Our Book's Intention

In this book I will be laying out some important matters to guide our thinking as we seek to engage politics as Christians. In each of the chapters we will look at both practical political issues as well as biblical principles that should govern our thinking.

In the first chapter I will lay down our foundation by noting that we must approach politics from a Christian perspective. But in order to do this we must have a Christian faith that is well-grounded. We must recognize the controlling framework within which we are to contemplate all political discussion and engage all political action. Thus, we must begin our study with the vitally important question of a Christian or biblical worldview. Too many Christians deem politics as a trivial matter of little concern to the Christian faith. Yet once we recognize what a worldview is all about, we will see the very real significance of our engaging in politics.

In the second chapter I will show how our nation was founded largely by Christians and generally on Christian principles. We will see how so many of our earliest documents tethered political actions to religious commitments. Though our Christian heritage is largely denied today, the historical documents tell otherwise. As Christians we need to understand that our faith impacted our nation in the past, and therefore can just as well impact it in the future. We must not forget the past if we are seeking to win the future.

The third chapter focuses on moral issues. I will show that by the very nature of the case politics necessarily involves morality. In the process we will see how only Christianity can provide a moral base for life — and politics. As we consider the general issue of morality, we will also look at a particular moral issue that is troubling our nation today: the homosexual revolution. We will note some of the dangers that this movement poses for our society and culture. These very real dangers call us to engage in politics.

In the fourth chapter I will show that a just and stable government created from within a Christian worldview must be built upon a secure foundation. We will see how our Constitution and the type of government it created were largely impacted by biblical covenantalism. As politically-concerned Christian citizens we must recognize the significance of our Constitution. It is an important means (under God's providence) whereby Americans have enjoyed large-scale and long-term safety, stability, liberty, and prosperity. Understanding the vital role of our Constitution in politics is crucial for engaging the political process — especially in a political setting that tends either to overlook the Constitution or re-work its meaning.

In the fifth chapter I will focus on one particularly important element of Christian-principled government: limited power. In our day of expansive governmental power, we must be aware of the biblical constraints God places on governments. Because of the very real dangers of totalitarianism, we as Christians must engage the political process to exercise our influence for limited government. I will note that not only does the Bible encourage governments of limited power, but our Constitution established a political structure that intentionally divided federal power into branches (diffused powers), with each given specific responsibilities (express powers) so that no branch has more power than the other branches (balanced powers).

The sixth chapter will concentrate on economic issues. Most people deem economics to be so boring that they have little interest in it. Yet we must make economic decisions every single day of our lives, as we buy this, forgo that, pay taxes on the other, and so forth. And government exercises a tremendous influence on economics. Though the Bible is not a formal textbook on economics, it nevertheless is filled with economic principles. These principles appear repeatedly in God's law as it estab-lishes economic rights, frequently in the prophets as they denounce economic oppression, often in Jesus' parables as he illustrates spiritual truths by economic realities, and much in the teachings of the Apostles as they confront economic sins. Clearly economic issues are not some sparsely discussed topic in Scripture. In our study we will consider the dangers of excessive indebtedness and heavy taxation, the importance of private property and the free market, as well as the morality of interest and investment.

As we come to the seventh chapter we will look into the matter of national defense. The Christian doctrine of sin that so motivated our forefathers in establishing our form of limited, constitutional govern-ment, arises as we consider another issue of great significance for politics: war. We will look into the legitimacy of war from a biblical per-spective, as well as Christian principles of a "just war." National defense obviously deals with the question of armed conflict among nations, but today national defense also involves border control and illegal immigration issues. So in this chapter I will briefly deal with the ques-tions of both military engagement and border security.

As we come to the conclusion of our study, in the eighth chapter I will deal with a tremendously important and very practical issue that faces us in every election. Because there are so few candidates operating on strongly-held biblical principles, and because they often have little chance of winning a general election, we find ourselves facing the question as to whether we should vote for "the lesser of evils." Politically-conservative voters — and especially, *Christian* conservative voters — have a particularly difficult time facing this prospect. But what does the Bible teach about such? In this chapter I will give practical, theological, and biblical consideration to the matter of lesser-evil voting.

## Chapter 1

# WORLDVIEW ANALYSIS

"We are destroying speculations and every lofty thing raised up against the knowledge of God, and we are taking every thought captive to the obedience of Christ." (2 Cor. 10:5)

In this book we will be considering politics from a Christian perspective. When we consider politics our Christian faith must be well-grounded. We must recognize the controlling framework within which we are to contemplate all political discussion and engage all political action. Thus, we must begin our study with the vitally important question of a Christian or biblical worldview.

A tragic fact of the evangelical Christian experience in America is that Hosea 4:6 well applies today: "My people are destroyed for lack of knowledge." We see this in the problem that too few Christians really understand what a worldview is and why a specifically *Christian* worldview is so vitally important. Consequently, as concerned evangelicals we must lament: "If the foundations are destroyed, / What can the righteous do?" (Psa. 11:3).

According to the American Religious Identity Survey 2008 report, 76% of Americans — more than three-quarters of the population — identify themselves as Christians.[1] Even more significantly, 34% of Americans even profess themselves to be "Born Again or Evangelical Christians." The real numbers behind these percentages show that 173,402,000 Americans claim to be Christians (p. 3), with 77,747,000 proclaiming themselves to be "born again" evangelicals. These are large numbers.

---

[1] On p. 2 of "The American Religious Identity Survey (ARIS 2008): Summary Report, March 2009" we read that this is "the third in a landmark series of large, nationally representative surveys that track changes in the religious loyalties of the U.S. adult population within the 48 contiguous states from 1990 to 2008." This Report was accessed on the Internet January, 2012: http://www. scribd. com/doc/17136871/American-Religious-Identification-Survey-ARIS-2008-Summary-Report.

Despite these large numbers, though, the impact of Christians on our society and culture is far less than we should expect. *Why*? Though we may discover several answers, I believe we can trace the problem to its root source: the superficial character of the modern Christian mind. Or as Mark Noll has called it: *The Scandal of the Evangelical Mind* (Eerdmans, 1995). Sadly, Christians today lack a basic understanding of the "whole counsel of God" (Acts 20:27 KJV); and therefore they quite naturally fail to engage a consistent reasoning process governed by God's counsel.

As evidence of this problem, we can simply note some polling data from the Barna Group, a leading research organization that focuses primarily on Christian ministries.[2] Their polling well explains the failure of current American Christian culture to more greatly impacting our social environment, cultural direction, and political order.

In March, 2009 the Barna Group published a poll showing that "overall, the current research revealed that only 9% of all American adults have a biblical worldview." This probably is not surprising in itself, but this poll also notes the startling fact regarding the biblical worldview that "even among born again adults, the statistics have remained flat: 18% in 1995, 22% in 2000, 21% in 2005, and 19% today." Ouch! Only 19% of born again Christians have a biblical worldview? That means 81% have defaulted to a *non*-biblical worldview.

Two further revelations from the Barna poll reflect the depth of this worldview deficiency. Shockingly, only 46% of "born again adults believe in absolute moral truth" and only 79% of born again Christians "believe that the Bible is accurate in all the principles it teaches." Clearly, God's people are being destroyed *within* by a debilitating "lack of knowledge" (Hos. 4:6). American Christians should look in a mirror and lament at their shallow reflection: "O, you of little faith" (Matt. 6:30; 8:26; 14:31; 16:8).

To make matters worse for the *long-term*, the problem is even deeper among young people as a category: "The research data showed that one pattern emerged loud and clear: young adults rarely possess a biblical worldview. The current study found that less than one-half of one percent of adults in the Mosaic generation – i.e., those aged 18 to 23 – have a biblical worldview." Not surprisingly, adult evangelicals lacking a Chris-

---

[2] "Barna Survey Examines Changes in Worldview Among Christians over the Past 13 Years." http://www.barna.org/barna-update/article/21-transformation/252-barna-survey-examines-changes-in-worldview-among-christians-over-the-past-13-years

tian worldview are producing young evangelicals having even less a commitment to worldview thinking. This should be expected in light of the biblical principle — which can operate as a two-edged sword: "Train up a child in the way he should go, / Even when he is old he will not depart from it" (Prov. 22:6). Apparently deficiently faithful parents are producing even less faithful children. We are operating as fallen Adam: "he became the father of a son in his own likeness, according to his image" (Gen. 5:3b).

The famed atheist philosopher and social critic Bertrand Russell (1872–1970) once perceptively stated: "Most Christians would die rather than think; in fact, they do." This is quite the opposite of the way things should be. Indeed, though Christians claim to hold the truth, rather than merely holding it, it should hold us.

But what *is* a Christian worldview? What are its biblical foundations? And does it apply in the political realm? If we are to rudely speak of politics and religion we must answer these questions.

### Technical Definition

Since Christians have such a deficient understanding of a worldview I will succinctly explain the matter under four headings. These should lead us ever more fully into a better understanding — *and self-conscious application* — of a Christian worldview. Those four headings are:

General definition of a worldview
Practical importance of a worldview
Various influences on a worldview
Specific explication of a worldview

Let us begin by considering a:

### General definition of a worldview

The core concept of a worldview may be expressed in a simple, one-sentence definition:

"A worldview is a conceptual framework through which we understand the world and our life in it."

We can easily see why this is a little more fully called: a "world-*and-life* view" in that it provides an organizing outlook on both our own lives as well as the world round about us.

Christian philosopher Greg Bahnsen provides us with a more technical and precise, but still rather succinct and manageable definition:

"A worldview is a network of presuppositions (which are not verified by the procedures of natural science) regarding reality (metaphysics), knowing (epistemology), and conduct (ethics) in terms of which every element of human experience is related and interpreted."[3]

(Fear not: below I will briefly explain the individual elements of this more technical definition.)

A worldview is significant in that we are human beings created in God's image (Gen. 1:26-27; 9:6; 1 Cor. 11:7; Jms. 3:9) and are thereby distinguished from animals. As images of God, we are rational beings that exercise a willful determination in impacting the world round about us. Therefore, we have a rational, conceptual outlook on the world and seek to make wise plans for our lives. Not only so, but God also created us as social creatures (Gen. 2:18), since we reflect him who is the ultimate society: he is a Trinity.[4]

Though we do operate in terms of a basic outlook on life, our world-view is not necessarily fully known, consciously framed, or carefully articulated. In fact, we may hold it unconsciously, thereby allowing it to be largely unrecognized, unintentional, and unrefined.

What is more, since we are finite (limited) and fallen (sinful) crea-tures, our worldview assumptions may be either true, partly true, or false. And since we are finite and fallen, our worldview may be either consistently or inconsistently employed in our daily lives. Indeed, sin generally insures that our worldview will be erratically engaged (cf. Matt. 26:33–34; Rom. 7:8–11, 14–20; Gal. 2:11–14). Yet, unless we suffer from some extreme delusional disorder or traumatic brain injury, as rational, willful, social beings we do operate in terms of *some* worldview.

Now we must move on to consider the:

---

[3] See: Gary DeMar, ed., *Pushing the Antithesis: The Apologetic Methodology of Greg L. Bahnsen* (Powder Springs, Geo.: American Vision, 2007), 42–43.

[4] In this regard we should note the creation account's record of God's inter-trinitarian communication. In Gen. 1:26 God says: "Let *Us* make man in *Our* image." God alone is the Creator (Gen. 1:1; Neh. 9:6; Acts 17:24; 1 Cor. 8:3; Rev 4:11), which also includes the Holy Spirit (Gen. 1:2; Psa. 104:30; Isa. 40:12–13), and Christ (John 1:3; Col. 1:15–16; Heb. 1:2). Angels are created beings, not creators.

## Practical importance of a worldview

As a big picture outlook on life, a worldview involves our basic, controlling assumptions about the world and our role in it. When rationally considered it formulates a comprehensive, integrated, and harmonious understanding of reality. It involves our basic presuppositions, thought processes, external actions, and even spontaneous reflexes in life. A worldview answers such questions as:

What is reality?
Why am I here?
Where am I going?
What is the meaning of life?
How do I know?
Are there moral absolutes?

Thus, a rational and recognized worldview is essential for us as wise and productive social beings. By rationally organizing the world round about us, it helps us insure our self-preservation, initiate daily actions, weigh personal decisions, make long-term plans, engage moral behavior, effect acceptable interaction, and so forth. So then, by the very nature of the case, a worldview is of enormous *practical* significance.

The presuppositions (basic assumptions) that underlie a worldview and which all men hold in one form or another, play a vital role in all human thought and behavior. The various presuppositions we hold govern the way we think and act all the way down to how we select and employ specific facts out of the constant stream of facts presented to us each moment of every day of entire lives. Basic, core presuppositions are the very foundation blocks upon which we conceive and operate in the world about us.

As a consequence of all of this, a consciously-held worldview must be founded on basic foundational ideas that we hold to be unchallengeable truth. We hold certain presuppositions about reality and build from there in our learning, communicating, behaving, planning, and so forth. A worldview necessarily exerts a powerful, practical influence over our life and conduct. It serves as our most basic decision-making filter, enabling us to make sense of the large and complex amount of information, experiences, relationships and opportunities we face in life. By helping to clarify what a person believes to be true, desirable, and important, a worldview has a dramatic influence on one's daily life.

At this stage of our analysis we must recognize the:

**Various influences on a worldview**

As we have been noting, all people are images of God and therefore have a worldview that is held either consciously or unconsciously. Unfortunately, too many people — including Christians — pick up much of their worldview subconsciously and therefore unreflectively and without challenge. We pick it up from the many social forces at work in our society and culture.

Since we live in a fallen world (Rom. 3:9, 23; Eph. 2:1–3; 1 John 5:19), we are under a constant and unrelenting barrage of temptations and influences from the sinful realities, spiritual forces, and secular ideas all around us (Eph. 2:1–3; 1 Tim. 6:9; Jms. 1:13–15). For instance, the great Apostle Paul even lamented:

> "For we know that the Law is spiritual, but I am of flesh, sold into bondage to sin. For what I am doing, I do not understand; for I am not practicing what I would like to do, but I am doing the very thing I hate. But if I do the very thing I do not want to do, I agree with the Law, confessing that the Law is good. So now, no longer am I the one doing it, but sin which dwells in me. For I know that nothing good dwells in me, that is, in my flesh; for the willing is present in me, but the doing of the good is not. For the good that I want, I do not do, but I practice the very evil that I do not want. But if I am doing the very thing I do not want, I am no longer the one doing it, but sin which dwells in me." (Rom. 7:14–20)

Because of this, we inadvertently absorb fallen, sinful principles by osmosis from our various friendships, personal associations, work environment, pleasure reading, the news media, television programing, movies, music, and many other avenues. Life is fraught with hidden dangers — which is why sin is often called "stumbling" (Matt. 5:9, 30; 18:6–9; Rom. 14:13, 21; 1 Cor. 8:9, 13; Jms. 2:10; 1 Jn 2:10). Indeed, James warns that "we all stumble in many ways" (Jms. 3:2).

Calling us away from such temptations, Jesus urges us to be "shrewd as serpents" as we live in this fallen world (Matt. 10:16). God's word calls upon us to "walk in the light" (1 Jn 2:7; cp. Job 29:3; Psa. 36:9; 89:15; Prov. 6:23). Indeed, it presents itself as that light: "Your word is a lamp to my feet / And a light to my path" (Psa. 119:105). Therefore, Paul directs us to live reflectively and wisely in this fallen world:

"Therefore be careful how you walk, not as unwise men but as wise, making the most of your time, because the days are evil. So then do not be foolish, but understand what the will of the Lord is." (Eph. 5:15–17)

"Conduct yourselves with wisdom toward outsiders, making the most of the opportunity. Let your speech always be with grace, as though seasoned with salt, so that you will know how you should respond to each person." (Col. 4:5–6)

He is urging us to live self-consciously Christian lives.

In order to do this, we must allow God's *word* to influence us:

"The law of the LORD is perfect, restoring the soul; / The testimony of the LORD is sure, making wise the simple. / The precepts of the LORD are right, rejoicing the heart; / The commandment of the LORD is pure, enlightening the eyes." (Psa. 19:7–8)

"Your commandments make me wiser than my enemies, / For they are ever mine. I have more insight than all my teachers, / For Your testimonies are my meditation. / I understand more than the aged, / Because I have observed Your precepts." (Psa. 119:98–100)

As believers we must recognize the fundamental contrast between the Christian and non-Christian worldviews. But since even we ourselves are born sinners, even our "natural" inclinations are *away* from God. Therefore, God's word warns us: "do not be wise in your own eyes" (Prov. 3:7). Indeed, it directs us: "trust in the LORD with all your heart / And do not lean on your own understanding" (Prov. 3:5).

Followers of Christ must understand the reality, enormity, and pervasiveness of sin, along with its impact on worldview thinking. When considering the Christian and the secular worldviews we are *not* comparing two systems of truth sharing a basically similar outlook with only intermittent differences at specific turns. *We are contrasting two whole, complete, and antithetical systems of thought.*

Because of the holistic nature of worldviews, each fact or piece of data presented either to the Christian or the non-Christian will be weighed, categorized, organized, and judged as to its possibility and significance in terms of the all pervasive worldview held by that person. And if that worldview is not implicitly, distinctively, and self-consciously Christian, it will exercise a negative influence on our thought and life.

But now let us make a:

**Specific explication of a worldview**

I would like now to backup to analyze Greg Bahnsen's semi-technical definition of a worldview. I will repeat it, then focus on its major statements. This will be so important for directing us self-consciously to incorporate a Christian worldview in our lives. Bahnsen's definition states that:

> "A worldview is a network of presuppositions (which are not verified by the procedures of natural science) regarding reality (metaphysics), knowing (epistemology), and conduct (ethics) in terms of which every element of human experience is related and interpreted."

Let us consider the individual elements in his statement.

First, "a worldview is a *network*." As we begin we must note that a worldview forms a wide-ranging network of presuppositions, an entire, *inter-related system* of assumptions about the world and life. This network is a *complex web* of *numerous beliefs* organized in an inter-locking, inter-dependent, self-contained truth system.

Unfortunately, most evangelical Christians generally think in a piece-meal fashion, focusing on a few stray individual doctrines rather than of a full-scale, co-ordinated system of beliefs. They tend to view the Christian faith as a random *assortment* of free-standing doctrines rather than as a coherent *system* of inter-locking truth claims. In fact, we even use the Bible thus, choosing verses out of context without recognizing they are part of a book.

Second, "a worldview is a network of *presuppositions*." A worldview — *any* worldview, whether Christian *or* secular — is really founded on *special kinds* of beliefs known as "presuppositions." This does not mean that it is established on just any collection of one's favorite beliefs, but rather on premises of a very important kind, known as "presuppositions."

But just what is a "presupposition"? Bahnsen carefully defines "presupposition" for us:

> "A 'presupposition' is an elementary assumption in one's reasoning or in the process by which opinions are formed. . . . [It] is not just any assumption in an argument, but a personal commitment that is held at the most basic level of one's network of beliefs. Presuppositions form a wide-ranging, foundational *perspective* (or starting point) in terms of which everything else is interpreted and evaluated. As such, presuppositions have the greatest authority in one's thinking, being treated as

one's least negotiable beliefs and being granted the highest immunity to revision."[5]

A presupposition is, therefore, an "elementary" (i.e., basic, foundational, starting point) assumption about reality as a whole. This elementary presupposition serves as an essential condition necessary to one's outlook on the world and life. It is a necessary precondition for human thought and experience, without which logical reasoning would be impossible and human experience unintelligible. Let me flesh this out a little more so that you can see the significance of your presuppositions.

Presuppositions are *hidden* assumptions that you *reflexively* depend upon for such fundamental issues of human experience as: the world (the nature and structure of reality: is there a real, physical world out there? Or is all an illusion or a dream?), knowledge (the possibility and method of knowledge: can things be truly known? Or is all subjective and ultimately unknowable?), and morality (the standards and universality of morality: are morals personal and arbitrary? Or are they objective and universal? Are they invariant? Or are they changing?). These basic presuppositions about the world and life guide you in understanding the world, discovering and resolving problems, planning for the future, living according to moral principles, and more.

Third, " a worldview is a network of presuppositions . . . in terms of which *all* experience is *related*." Christians are not the only ones holding a worldview, as if this were some sort of narrowly religious conception. *Every* sane person must have — *does* have! — a framework which relates his experiences into a systematic whole, so that he may ably live in the world and recognize his relationship to it. Everyone necessarily has a particular way of looking at the world which serves to organize ideas about the world in his mind. Any rational act *by definition* operates in terms of a particular understanding of the world, a particular worldview.

Fourth, "a worldview is a network of presuppositions . . . in terms of which all experience is related *and interpreted*." Presuppositions hold the highest level of authority in one's worldview and are the basis by which we interpret and understand reality. Consequently, they are the convictions you are least likely to give up. In his book *Always Ready*, Bahnsen explains the situation:

---

[5] Greg L. Bahnsen, *Van Til's Apologetic: Readings and Analysis* (Phillipsburg, N.J.: Presbyterian and Reformed, 1998), 2, n4.

"Every thinker grants preferred status to *some* of his beliefs and the linguistic assertions which express them. These privileged convictions are 'central' to his 'web of beliefs,' being treated as immune from revision — until the network of convictions itself is altered. . . . The reality of human nature and behavior should be recognized: our thoughts, reasoning and conduct are governed by presuppositional convictions which are matters of deep personal concern, which are far from vacuous or trivial, and to which we intend to intellectually cling and defend 'to the end.'"[6]

By the very nature of the case your worldview — *everyone's* worldview, even the unbeliever's — must be founded on basic presupposed ideas held as truth and which are immune from revision. Men must necessarily begin with these presuppositions and build from there in learning, communicating, behaving, planning, and so forth. Presuppositions provide the authoritative standards by which we evaluate life issues.

Living in the world but lacking an interpretive worldview (which is impossible for the sane) would be like reading a Bible verse for the first time and without any context. Consider one verse that never serves as any Christian's "life verse." 1 Chronicles 26:18 (KJV) reads: "At Parbar westward, four at the causeway, and two at Parbar." This verse is virtually unintelligible apart from its contextual setting.

Or we may use a movie that functions as a comic allegory on worldview: In *The Gods Must be Crazy* a small tribe of African bushmen are confronted by a Coke bottle tossed out of small plane flying overhead. They not only develop strange ideas about the meaning and significance of the bottle (what is it, where did it come from, and why is it here?), but one of them determines to take it to the edge of the world and throw it back to the gods. As he travels to do so, he runs into modern civilization and is absolutely confused about the meaning of the various things he encounters. He has no interpretive framework to properly understand the new world he experiences. Similarly, a worldview gives meaningful context to the facts of the world and life.

Fifth, "a worldview is a network of presuppositions which are not tested by natural science." Presuppositions cannot be counted, weighed,

---

[6] Greg L. Bahnsen, *Always Ready: Directions for Defending the Faith*, ed. by Robert R. Booth (Atlanta: American Vision, 1996), 218.

or measured; they are not seen, heard, or felt. But they are the very foundations upon which science stands and sensory experiences are understood. Just as the scientist stands on the floor of a laboratory to perform his experiments, so science itself stands on the floor of presuppositions in order to analyze the world.

In our materialistic world today, many people either denigrate or deny altogether non-material issues. They prefer that which is "more real" (objective, external). But they must understand the rules of logic, issues of morality, conceptions of love, and so forth are fundamentally important immaterial realities. As rational creatures we must understand the significance of these unseen realities — for they are foundational to human life and experience.

Christians, it is important that you realize that Christian faith is a worldview. And therefore Christian worldview considerations require that if you are committed to Christ in one particular area of life (say, the inner-personal life), you must be committed to him at every point in life (including in employment, academics, entertainment, law, science, politics, whatever). Christianity is not concerned merely with a narrow range of human experience, involving only your prayer life, devotional reading, pubic worship, or family relations.

The biblical declaration "Jesus is Lord" (Rom. 10:9; cp. Acts 16:31; 1 Cor. 12:3; Phil. 2:11) requires that you submit to him in all areas of life. Too many believers are "Sunday-only" Christians who quarantine religious faith from the "real" issues of every day life and experience in the workaday world.

Since Christianity is a world-and-life view, it has a distinctive approach to reasoning, human nature, social relations, education, recreation, economics, art, industry, medicine, and every other human endeavor — including, as we shall see, politics. To be truly committed to Christ within the very heart of your life requires that you be committed to Christ throughout the very whole of your life.

Therefore, Scripture pits Christian worldview thinking over against non-Christian thinking. Two worldviews are in collision; they are not simply two variations of similar themes. Thus, we are warned to "see to it that no one takes you captive through philosophy and empty deception, according to the tradition of men, according to the elementary principles of the world, rather than according to Christ" (Col. 2:8).

Paul even authoritatively commands us:

"So this I say, and affirm together with the Lord, that you walk no longer just as the Gentiles also walk, in the futility of their mind, being darkened in their understanding, excluded from the life of God because of the ignorance that is in them, because of the hardness of their heart. ... Be renewed in the spirit of your mind, and put on the new self, which in the likeness of God has been created in righteousness and holiness of the truth." (Eph. 4:17–18, 23)

He directs us to: "not be conformed to this world, but be transformed by the renewing of your mind, so that you may prove what the will of God is, that which is good and acceptable and perfect." (Rom. 12:2)

But now let us consider a worldview's:

### Biblical Foundation

I do not have space to fully flesh out a worldview and all of its implications. Yet I believe it is important that we at least recognize some of the basic elements of a distinctively Christian worldview — especially as it impacts our understanding of history. After all, politics impacts the very flow and governance of history by men as social creatures.

The essential presuppositions undergirding the Christian worldview and its view of history include the following key concepts: God, creation, providence, fall, redemption, revelation, and consummation.

*God.* A proper view of history, its meaning, and purpose requires a proper view of God. God exists and is absolutely independent and wholly self-sufficient. In Exodus 3:14 he defines himself by his special covenantal name "YHWH" ("Yahweh / Jehovah"). This is his name "forever" (Exo. 3:15). It is so prominent that the Scriptures can simply mention "the name" (Lev. 24:11, 16). God jealously establishes a fundamental moral law that his name must not be used in vain (Exo. 20:7; Deut. 5:11). In Exodus 3:14 he identifies himself as: "I am that I am." This self-designation is peculiarly important to our understanding of God. This name-statement is found in the imperfect tense in Hebrew, thereby emphasizing a constantly manifested quality.

From this name we may discern certain of God's intrinsic qualities: (1) His self-sufficiency: God exists of himself. He is wholly uncreated and self-existent. There is no principle or fact back of God accounting for his existence: "the Father has life in Himself" (John 5:26; Acts 17:25; cp. Isa. 40:20–25). Indeed, "in the beginning God" (Gen. 1:1a) — for he "created all things" (Eph. 3:9). (2) His eternity: he is of unlimited, eternal duration. The combination of the verb tense (imperfect) and its repetition ("I am"

/ "I am") emphasize his uninterrupted, continuous existence. Indeed, "from everlasting to everlasting, Thou art God" (Psa. 90:2; cp. Psa. 93:1–2; Isa. 40:28; 57:15).

(3) His sovereignty: he is absolutely self-determinative. He determines whatever he wills from within his own being. He can declare absolutely "I am that I am," without fear of any overpowering entity or countervailing force to challenge him. As the Absolute One he operates with unfettered liberty. He is not conditioned by outward circumstance. He is what he is because he is what he is. He is completely self-definitional and has no need of anything outside of himself (Isa. 40:9–31), for "I am God, and there is no one like Me" (Exo. 9:14; cp. Isa. 44:7; Jer. 50:44).

(4) His immutability: he declares "I, the LORD, do not change" (Mal. 3:6). He is forever the same, for in him "there is no variation, or shifting shadow" (Jms. 1:17). Thus, we can trust that he will not change his mind or his plan in governing history, for "God is not a man, / that He should lie, / Nor a son of man, / that He should repent; / Has He said, and will He not do it? / Or had He spoken, and will / He not make it good?" (Num. 23:19).

*Creation.* All of reality derives from a personal, moral, sovereign being: the God of Scripture. Scripture powerfully declares that "there is but one God, the Father, from whom are all things and we exist for Him; and one Lord, Jesus Christ, by whom are all things, and we exist through Him" (1 Cor. 8:6). All things of all sorts were created by him (John 1:3; Col. 1:16).

The Christian's creational viewpoint puts man under God and over nature (Gen. 1:26–27; Psa. 8). It imparts transcendent (higher) meaning to temporal history and sets before man a high calling. The entire universe from the smallest atomic particle to the largest and farthest flung galaxy was created out of nothing. It exists solely by the exercise of God's creative will, and was brought into being by his sovereign, successive, spoken commands (Gen. 1:1; Exo. 20:11; Heb. 11:3). All facts and laws, all people and materials, trace their origin, meaning, and purpose back to God.

The Christian faith is concerned with the material world, the here and now. The Christian interest in the material here-and-now is evident in that: (1) God created the earth and man's body as material entities, and all "very good" (Gen. 1:1–31; 2:7). (2) The Son of God took upon himself a true, material human body in order to redeem man (Rom. 1:3; 9:5; 1 John 4:1–3). (3) God's word directs us how to live in the present, material world (Rom. 12:1–2; Eph. 5:15–17; 2 Tim. 3:16–17). (4) God intends for us to remain on the earth for our fleshly sojourn, and does not remove us upon our being saved by his grace (John 17:15; Job 14:5; 2 Cor. 5:9–10). Thus, prior to our ultimate destination in the eternal state, we must recognize the truth that all men live before God in the material world (2 Chron. 16:9; Psa. 33:13–15; Prov. 15:3; Acts 17:28; Heb. 4:13), which he has created for his own glory, as the place of man's habitation (Psa. 24:1; 115:16; Prov. 15:3; Dan. 5:23; Acts 25:24–31; Rev 4:11).

*Providence*. God has an eternally-decreed, sovereignly-determined plan for the Universe. He personally and intimately administers this plan for his own glory. Providence imparts transcendent meaning into the flow and direction of history. God "works all things after the counsel of His will" (Eph. 1:11; cf. Psa. 33:11; Isa. 45:10–11); he "causes all things to work together" (Rom. 8:28a). Christ himself is before all things, and by means of him all things hold together or cohere (John 1:1; Col. 1:17). He carries along or upholds all things by the word of his power (Heb. 1:3). Providence in the Christian worldview is the alternative to Chance in the non-Christian worldview.

*Fall*. Because of God's testing of Adam, which results in Adam's Fall (Gen. 3:1–8), history becomes the battleground of Christ and Satan (Gen. 3:15). Sin affects every aspect of human endeavor, distorting all of reality. We cannot understand our historical situation apart from the intrusion of sin, as an unnatural factor. Neither may we think of man's fundamental problem as related to his being finite. In fact, finite Adam's pre-Fall abilities were remarkable (Gen. 2:15, 19–20), as will be our resurrected existence (1 Cor. 15:42–53). Rather man's fundamental problem is ethical, related to his rebellion against God and his Law-word (Gen. 3:1–7; Rom. 1:18–23; 5:10; 8:7–8). Because of this he labors under God's curse (Gen. 3:14–15; Rom. 5:12–19; Gal. 3:10).

But God does not abandon history because of man's Fall. Instead, history witnesses the rising of a new factor to compensate for the fall:

*Redemption*. A major force in history is God's redemptive activity in reconciling creation back to himself (Gen. 3:15; Col. 1:19–23). God establishes his redemptive plan in order to bring wayward man back to himself. "God did not send the Son into the world to judge the world, but that the world should be saved through Him" (John 3:17). In fact, "the Son of God appeared for this purpose, to destroy the works of the devil" (1 John 3:8). We can possess no proper understanding of historical progress and political hope when considering only the Fall of man. We must take into account also God's restorative acts in redemption.

*Revelation.* God reveals himself and various aspects of his will infallibly and inerrantly in his holy word, the Bible: "All Scripture is inspired by God . . . so that the man of God may be adequate, equipped for every good work" (2 Tim. 3:16; cp. John 10:35; 2 Pet. 1:20, 21). God's causative, creative word is also his providential, governing word. God's eternal decree, from which his prophetic word springs into history, is neither abstract nor random; it is concrete and rational. It is not raw, brute force, but wise, structured power. God's word intelligibly constructs all things, "declaring the end from the beginning" (Isa. 46:10; cp. Psa. 33:11; 148:5; Heb. 1:3; 11:3). God's objective revelation in Scripture is foundational to a truly Christian political hope.

*Consummation.* Not only does history have a beginning, not only does God providentially guide it, but he does so toward a particular end: "He has fixed a day in which He will judge the world in righteousness" (Acts 17:31; cp. Isa. 46:10; 55:11). Our labor on earth "is not in vain in the Lord" (1 Cor. 15:58). We labor in the present with a view to the future — and ultimately to history's consummation and the eternal state. "For our citizenship is in heaven, from which also we eagerly wait for a Savior, the Lord Jesus Christ; who will transform the body of our humble state into conformity with the body of his glory, by the exertion of the power that He has even to subject all things to Himself" (Phil. 3:20–21). We labor in the light of God's victory, not in the darkness of the unknown.

The dark, unbelieving worldview of humanism is well-captured by the atheist philosopher Bertrand Russell (1872–1970):

> Even more purposeless, more void of meaning, is the world which Science presents for our belief. Amid such a world, if anywhere, our ideals henceforward must find a home. That Man is the product of causes which had no prevision of the end they were achieving; that his origin, his growth, his hopes and fears, his loves and his beliefs, are but the outcome of accidental collocations of atoms; that no fire, no heroism, no intensity of thought and feeling, can preserve an individual life beyond the grave; that all the labours of the ages, all the devotion, all the inspiration, all the noonday brightness of human genius, are destined to extinction in the vast death of the solar system, and that the whole temple of Man's achievement must inevitably be buried beneath the debris of a universe in ruins — all these things, if not quite beyond dispute, are yet so nearly certain, that no philosophy which rejects them can hope to stand. Only within the scaffolding of these truths, only on

the firm foundation of unyielding despair, can the soul's habitation henceforth be safely built.[7]

I can afford no more space to this important matter of the philosophy of history. But it should be evident that whether or not the entire course of world history is under the absolute, sovereign administration of the infinitely personal God of Scripture means everything to the Christian worldview. Whether or not we view the universe as God's creation designed for his glory is fundamentally important. If God is not absolutely sovereign, some competing god or some countervailing principle or some unforeseen fortuity could throw a dark blanket of obscurity over the ultimate eschatological outcome of universal history and human existence. This would undermine any hope for our spiritual and moral influence in history, thereby undercutting any Christian political hopes.

This leads us to our final point regarding a Christian worldview, the very purpose of this book. So now let us consider the Christian worldview's:

## Political Application

By the very nature of the case, a worldview must involve the "world." And a *Christian* worldview must therefore engage a *Christian* view of the world. And since politics is a large function in human society, you would think all Christians would recognize the importance of a Christian involvement in politics. But you would be wrong.

Many Christians discourage engagement in politics. In fact, they often attempt to use the Scripture to dissuade Christians from political endeavors and concerns. Others simply avoid political issues for one reason or another. Some of the leading complaints against a concern with or an involvement in politics are the following:

*The fear of man*: "Politics involves power, and power corrupts. Thus, Christians should steer clear of politics as fraught with danger." But by following this principle Christians leave this power in the hands of corrupted men — corrupted men who often seek to suppress the Christian faith in culture. Furthermore, as I showed above sinful temptation surrounds us everywhere in the world: should we avoid everything as dangerous?

---

[7] This is from Bertrand Russell's most famous essay, "A Free Man's Worship." http://users.drew.edu/~jlenz/br-fmw.html

*Politics is dirty*: As facetiously noted in the introduction to this chapter, it is unfortunate that 90% of politicians give the other 10% a bad name. But who is going to clean up politics if Christians refuse? Proverbs 29:2 teaches us: "When the righteous increase, the people rejoice, / But when a wicked man rules, people groan." Perhaps politics is dirty because too many Christians have withdrawn from this endeavor. Christians should get involved in politics to correct this problem. John the Baptist did not encourage Roman soldiers to resign their commissions because of the abuses of the military; instead he urged them to conduct themselves morally within the system: "some soldiers were questioning him, saying, 'And what about us, what shall we do?' And he said to them, 'Do not take money from anyone by force, or accuse anyone falsely, and be content with your wages'" (Luke 3:14).

*Politics diverts money from the gospel*: "The money spent on political issues should be spent on evangelism and missions." But we see in oppressive governments overseas and even in frequent American laws that politics has the power to curtail and suppress Christian ministries if left unchecked by Christian influence. Without Christian participation and representation in the political process, our religious liberties will gradually evaporate. How can we stand apart from the political process?

The political and social trends of the last generation should offer clear warnings that freedom and liberty require diligent care and attention — especially by the Christian community (see ch. 3 below for the moral dangers of withdrawal). Furthermore, using this line of reasoning, virtually all human endeavors should be stopped so that the money could be used for missions — including education, retirement planning, buying cars, vacations, home decorating, and so forth. Consider how much you actually spend on things "of this world" as compared to how much you give to gospel ministries.

*Victory in politics is hopeless*: "Why get involved since we know we are going to lose?" J. Vernon McGee (1904–1988) famously complained: "Why polish brass on a sinking ship?" But this attitude actually becomes a self-fulfilling prophecy. And you are certainly not going to win if you *do not* get involved. The huge number of Christians in America need to be motivated, not discouraged.

*Christ is coming soon, so we should not waste our time on the affairs of the world*: "Since Christ is coming soon, why get involved in seeking long-term political solutions to social problems?" But Christians have been predicting Christ's return for centuries. Besides, are we not supposed to seek to promote the good regardless of how long we have to do it? And logically, should this principle not encourage us to forgo getting an education and saving for retirement?

*The principle of the separation of church and state should warn Christians away from politics*: "If Christians engage in politics, we will be breaching a fundamental principle of American government." But this is wrong in itself, for the First Amendment to the Constitution (1) forbids *Congress* from creating an established church (as Britain and most of the American colonies had when the Constitution was written) and (2) expressly "prohibits the free exercise" of religion (which politically-concerned Christians seek). Though we believe in the *institutional* separation of church and state, we do not believe in the separation of God from state.

*God calls us to separate from the world*: "Since God commands us to 'come out from among them and be separate,' we should not engage in politics. Rather we should demonstrate in our lives how Christianity is distinct from the world." But this interpretation of 2 Corinthians 6:17 is wrong, and if applied across the board would have Christians live in communes, wholly separated from our culture.

On and on I could go. You have heard these before. But by way of example let us consider one Christian website that vigorously warns against Christians engaging in the political process.[8] It even attempts to use Scripture to support this position.

> "One reason why so many wage an ineffective spiritual warfare, not being able to 'fight the good fight of faith,' is entanglements. This world system dangles before every Christian various spider-webs of entanglement, and politics is one of those."
>
> . . .
>
> "1 John 2:15 instructs us, 'Love not the world, neither the things that are in the world.' This is violated by those who give themselves to politics. It is never our responsibility to help the world system nor much less to love it."
>
> . . .
>
> "The Lord Jesus' words to Pilate are full of meaning for us: 'My kingdom is not of this world, else would my servants fight' (John 18:36). Since we are questioning them about "Christian" political involvement, they will have to give us some New Testament verses, teaching of the Lord or his

---

[8] http://www.lifehouse.org/tracts/thechristianandpolitics.htm.

apostles, that clearly and unmistakably teach Christians to become involved in any way in politics. Oops — there are none!"

So, despite this website and others of like mind, let us consider the Christian worldview and its call to political engagement. Does the Bible "clearly and unmistakably teach Christians to become involved in any way in politics"? I believe it does, and I will present this under five headings:

The Creation Mandate Expects It

God's Word Commands It

Biblical Examples Encourage It

Christ's Victory Secures It

God's Calling Requires It

Our Predicament Demands It

## The Creation Mandate expects it

The Creation Mandate appears in Genesis 1:26–28. It reads:

> "Then God said, 'Let Us make man in Our image, according to Our likeness; and let them rule over the fish of the sea and over the birds of the sky and over the cattle and over all the earth, and over every creeping thing that creeps on the earth.' God created man in His own image, in the image of God He created him; male and female He created them. God blessed them; and God said to them, 'Be fruitful and multiply, and fill the earth, and subdue it; and rule over the fish of the sea and over the birds of the sky and over every living thing that moves on the earth.'"

God gives this Mandate in the very context of his creating man on the earth. In fact, the Mandate defines man and explains his God-ordained purpose in creation. In so doing, it serves an important function in the creation record: it distinguishes mankind from the animal, plant, and protist kingdoms for: only man is created in "the image of God" (Gen. 1:26–27), a little lower than the angels (Psa. 8:5).

One vital function of this image is important for the question of political engagement: man's exercising dominion over the earth and under God. As is evident in their close relation in Genesis 1:26, the *dominion drive* ("let them rule") is a key aspect of man's being God's image ("Let us make man in Our image"). Thus, as God rules all things sovereignly,[9] man as his image mirrors his rule in the realm where he places him.

In this Mandate we see that man has both (1) a basic constitutional *urge* to dominion as a result of his being *created* in God's image and (2) a fundamental *responsibility* to do so as a result of his being *commanded* by God's decree. Man's distinctive, God-given task in the world is to develop culture. Culture may be defined as the sum deposit of the normative labors of man over time. Adam was to "cultivate" the world (Gen. 1:26–28), beginning in Eden (Gen. 2:15).

We see clear biblical evidence that early, post-fall man is driven to cultural exploits well beyond the expectations of humanistic anthropologists and sociologists. Thus, very early in history we see the effect and significance of the Creation Mandate among Adam's offspring. Early man instinctively acts as a dominical creature, subduing the earth and developing culture. He is no knuckle-dragging, "what me worry?," Neanderthal. Rather he is a high-order, intelligent image of God who quickly develops foundational aspects of human social culture by entering into marriage (Gen. 2:23–25; 4:1, 19, 25; cp. Matt. 19:4–5), farming (Gen. 2:15; 3:18, 23; 4:2, 12), wearing clothes (Gen. 3:21), engaging in religious worship (Gen. 4:3–4), establishing cities (Gen. 4:17), raising livestock (Gen. 4:2, 20), creating music and musical instruments (Gen. 4:21), crafting tools from metal (Gen. 4:22), and so forth.

In that man is a social creature (Gen. 2:18; 4:17), his culture-building necessarily includes the political order. We see this actually applied in his establishing a "city" (an organized community) in Genesis 4:17, which by the very nature of the case requires some sort of governmental oversight. So then, from the very moment of his creation, God not only commands man to develop all of creation, but man actually begins to do so. Culture is not the accidental result of a long, slow evolutionary process within the historical order. Neither should cultural development, including political governance, be accidental to the Christian enterprise.

Despite the assumption of some Christians, we must realize that God does *not* withdraw the Creation mandate when man falls into sin. It is

---

[9] God exercised his ultimate authority by creating all things (Gen. 1:1, 31; cp 1:3, 6, 7, 9, 11, 14a, 16, 20, 2, 24, 25, 28), naming them (Gen. 1:5, 8, 10), establishing their places (Gen. 1:6a, 7, 9, 11, 14, 17, 20, 24, 28), and designating their functions (Gen. 1:4, 6b, 11, 14b, 16, 18, 26–27). Man reflects God in being a ruler over creation (Gen. 1:26–27) and naming the animals (Gen. 2:19–20).

expressly reiterated in several places in Scripture *after* the Fall, as we see in Genesis 9:1–3, Psalm 8:4–8, and Hebrews 2:6–8. Nevertheless, the intruding factor of sin does necessitate divine intervention and the supplementation of the original Mandate with a new factor: *redemption*.

Immediately upon Adam's fall into sin (Gen. 3:1–7), God graciously acts by providing for man's salvation. Genesis 3:15 promises the coming of a Redeemer ("the seed of the woman"), who will destroy Satan ("the seed of the serpent"). This verse is often called the "protoevangelium," which means the "first promise of the gospel." The gospel of God's saving grace begins at this point in history. Because of this, Romans 1:1–2, 16:25–27, Galatians 3:8, and Hebrews 4:2 can speak of the "gospel" existing in the Old Testament.

Thus, we see that government is divinely ordained for man as created in God's image to rule. In fact, Scripture presents us with four foundational authority structures: (1) self-government (Gen. 2:16–17; 4:7; 1 Pet. 1:15–16); (2) family government (Gen. 1:26–28; 2:24; 3:16; Eph. 5:22–6:4; 1 Tim. 5:8); (3) church government (Heb. 13:17; cp. 1 Cor. 16:15–16), and (4) civil government (Gen. 9:5–6; Rom. 13:1–4; 1 Pet. 2:13–14). As Christians recognizing the significance of a holistic worldview, we must take an interest in and bring God's word to bear upon all levels of authority, including politics.

Furthermore, regarding the Christian worldview and our political obligation, we must note that:

### God's word commands it

As just noted, in the Creation Mandate God establishes man as a dominical creature over the whole earthly realm — which necessarily involves politics. As the psalmist says: "The heavens are the heavens of the Lord, / But the earth He has given to the sons of men" (Psa. 115:16)

Now let us take a step further. Let us remember that God establishes Israel as a *nation* in her own land. We can see this especially in Deuteronomy, which prepares Israel for her soon-coming entry into the Promised Land (Deut. 1:8, 19–21; 3:28; cp. Josh. 3:17; 4:1). She will soon be transitioning from a large people-group to a settled nation status. And as she does so, God himself will give her political and judicial laws to govern her national life (Deut. 4:1, 14, 40; 5:1, 31; 6:1; 7:11; etc.). Politics, then, is a part of God's law for his people Israel.

Not only so, but one of God's expressly-stated (revealed!) purposes for his establishing Israel as a nation under his Law is instructive for our worldview application. He gives her statutes and laws *so that* she might serve as an *example* to the governments of the world regarding a *proper political-order*:

> "See, I have taught you statutes and judgments just as the Lord my God commanded me, that you should do thus in the land where you are entering to possess it. So keep and do them, for that is your wisdom and your understanding in the sight of the peoples who will hear all these statutes and say, 'Surely this great nation is a wise and understanding people.' For what great nation is there that has a god so near to it as is the Lord our God whenever we call on Him? Or what great nation is there that has statutes and judgments as righteous as this whole law which I am setting before you today?" (Deut. 4:5–8; cp. Isa. 24:5; 51:4; Psa. 2:9-10; 119:118)

If the other nations are to praise Israel for her "statutes and judgments," surely they are to *emulate them* in their own governments. And if both God's people Israel and the other nations of the world are to establish such praiseworthy "statutes and judgments," we have another strong witness to the Bible's interest in politics. How then can the Christian be disinterested?

Elsewhere in Scripture we find positive declarations regarding politics. In 2 Samuel 23:3 we learn that "he who rules over men righteously" is the one "who rules in the fear of God." Political rule can — and *should* be — a righteous rule. This requires that righteous people become involved.

In 2 Chronicles 19:6–7 judges are called upon to make a judgment "for the LORD" and to "let the fear of the LORD" be upon them. Politics should operate in the fear of the LORD — which requires Christian involvement.

In Psalm 2:10–12 the kings and judges of the world are to "show discernment" and "take warning" about how they rule. If they do so, they will be blessed of the Lord. They must also praise the Lord in their callings (Psa. 148:1, 11). How can politics be something that the righteous should avoid?

In the New Testament we learn that God ordains civil government and that he intends that civil magistrates function as "ministers of God" who must execute God's wrath upon evil doers:

"Every person is to be in subjection to the governing authorities. For there is no authority except from God, and those which exist are established by God. Therefore whoever resists authority has opposed the ordinance of God; and they who have opposed will receive condemnation upon themselves. For rulers are not a cause of fear for good behavior, but for evil. Do you want to have no fear of authority? Do what is good and you will have praise from the same; for it is a minister of God to you for good. But if you do what is evil, be afraid; for it does not bear the sword for nothing; for it is a minister of God, an avenger who brings wrath on the one who practices evil." (Rom. 13:1–4)

So if God himself ordains civil authority, appoints its members to function as "ministers of God," who are to execute his wrath upon evil doers, how can Christians say that we should avoid politics? If we do so, we must avoid applying a portion of Scripture. We would merely affirm the "partial counsel of God," you might say.

We should note also that any retreat from political issues or avoiding them would not be in accord with biblical precedent. Joseph rose to the highest ranking official under Pharaoh in Egypt (Gen. 41:37–45; 42:5; 45:8–9). Moses led Israel to freedom from Egyptian bondage (Exo. 8:1; 12ff; Heb. 11:27–29). Daniel advised King Nebuchadnezzar of Babylon regarding what he should do in office (Dan. 4:27). Nehemiah was cupbearer to Artaxerxes , the Persian king (Neh. 1:11), and Mordecai "was second only to King Ahasuerus" (Esth. 10:3).

The Old Testament prophets frequently critiqued foreign powers for their abuses. Isaiah rebuked Babylon, Moab, Damascus, Ethiopia, and Egypt (Isa. 13–23). Jeremiah challenged Egypt, Moab, Ammon, Damascus, and Babylon (Jer. 46–51). Ezekiel denounced Ammon, Moab, Edom, Philistia, and Tyre (Eze. 25–32). Amos prophesied against Damascus, Gaza, Tyre, Edom, Ammon, and Moab (Amos 1–2). We see the same tendencies in Obadiah, Jonah, Nahum, Habakkuk 2, and Zephaniah 2.

Both John the Baptist and Christ speaks out against civil authorities for their immoral conduct (Matt. 14:1–12; Mark 6:18; Luke 13:32). Christ challenges Caesar's claim to worship, while allowing his right to taxation (Matt. 22:15–21). Paul reasoned with the Roman governor Felix about righteousness in such a way that Felix became frightened (Acts 24:25). The Apostle John presents the Emperor Nero (the sixth "king" of the Roman empire) as a great and dangerous "beast" (Rev 13:1; 17:9–10). Regarding civil authorities, Scripture encourages our prayer for them

(Ezra 6:10; Psa. 72:1; Jer. 29:7; 1 Tim. 2:2) and our honoring them (Rom. 13:7; 1 Pet. 2:17).

Despite the general call to submit to civil rulers, the Christian must at all times hold God and Christ as supreme authority. Consequently, occasions can arise wherein the Christian must refuse any governmental directive which would obligate his doing that which is contrary to God's revealed will. The government may not act as God (Matt. 22:21; Acts 12:22–23; 20:20–23; cp. Isa. 14:4, 11–13; Eze. 28:1–3). It does not possess unimpeachable authority (Exo. 1:15–20; Dan. 3:8–30; Acts 5:29). Only Christ has "all authority in heaven and on earth" to command us (Matt. 28:18).

All of this now leads me to observe regarding the Christian's worldview, that:

### Christ's victory secures it

The Lord gives his "great commission" after his resurrection from the dead:

> "Jesus came up and spoke to them, saying, 'All authority has been given to Me in heaven and on earth. 'Go therefore and make disciples of all the nations, baptizing them in the name of the Father and the Son and the Holy Spirit, teaching them to observe all that I commanded you; and lo, I am with you always, even to the end of the age.'" (Matt. 28:18–20)

Notice, Christ's prefacing the actual commission with a bold claim: "All authority has been given to Me in heaven and on earth." This is a universal declaration that encompasses *all* authority — not only "in heaven" (spiritual matters) but "on earth" (temporal matters) Thus, his newly bestowed authority is identical with God the Father's, who is "Possessor of heaven and earth" (Gen. 14:19) and "Lord of heaven and earth" (Matt. 11:25). As a universal authority on the level with God's authority (who gives "statutes and judgments" for Israel and the nations), Christ's must include *political* authority.

Indeed, Christ's authority *does* impact the political order, for he is called "King of kings, and Lord of lords" (Rev. 19:16; cp. 17:14). Three other powerful New Testament verses that confirm this political implication are:

"He raised Him from the dead and seated Him at His right hand in the heavenly places, far above all rule and authority and power and dominion, and every name that is named." (Eph. 1:20–21a)

"For this reason also, God highly exalted Him, and bestowed on Him the name which is above every name." (Phil. 2:9)

"Who is at the right hand of God, having gone into heaven, after angels and authorities and powers had been subjected to Him." (1 Pet. 3:22)

Not only is Christ's authority above all others (kings, emperors, presidents), but it penetrates *every* realm. It is not just in the spiritual arena (the inner-personal realm), but in all spheres of life. His authority universally and comprehensively serves as the basis for a truly Christian worldview. The "all" which defines "authority" is here used in the distributive sense, entailing every form of authority. That is, each and every realm of thought and activity is under his authoritative command: ecclesial, familial, and personal — as well as ethical, social, cultural, financial, and every other realm, including the judicial, legal, and political realms. The rich reward of his redemptive labor is his appointment ("has been given," Matt. 28:18; cp. Acts 2:36; Rom. 1:3; Phil. 2:9) to sovereign lordship over all areas of life and thought.

On the basis of this universal authority, Christ commissions his disciples (and us today, for he is with his people "even to the end of the age," Matt. 28:20b): "Go therefore and make disciples of all the nations" (Matt. 28:19a). This fits well with his world-encompassing authority. The ascended Christ directs his people to promote and expand his kingdom in the world. Would he assert his sovereign lordship so vigorously and command his people so majestically if we were supposed to avoid political matters?

The word "nations" here is significant for our worldview application regarding politics. It is the Greek word *ethnos*. Etymologists widely agree that it was derived from another Greek word, *ethos*, which means "'mass' or 'host' or 'multitude' bound by the same manners, customs and other distinctive features."[10] Thus, Jesus is not merely calling us to disciple *individuals* (though it surely must begin there). Rather, he calls for our

---

[10] Karl Ludwig Schmidt, "*ethnos*" in Gerhard Kittle, ed., *Theological Dictionary of the New Testament,* trans. by Geoffery W. Bromiley (Grand Rapids: Eerdmans, 1964), 2:369.

discipling "all the nations" (*ethnos*), involving men as individuals united together in all their socio-cultural labors and relations.

Consequently, we must have a concern for the governments of the nations as an important aspect of culture. The call to "disciple the nations" involves actively and diligently setting forth Christ's claims even upon governments (cp. Matt. 10:18; Acts 9:15). To pietistically omit concern for civil government is to truncate the implications of the Great Commission. It is to rework Jesus claim to read: "most authority has been given to me."

Let us now note regarding the political implications of the Christian worldview, that:

### God's calling requires it

In light of all that we have studied, it should be obvious that God's calling upon our lives includes our concern and involvement in political issues: After all, he created us in his image and commanded us to rule over the world; he established a government in Israel, which he intended to be a model for the nations; and his Great Commission claims "all authority" both in heaven *and* "on earth," while commissioning us to disciple all the cultures of the world ("nations"). So now let us consider a few select verses that show God's calling on Christians to engage every area of life — including the political realm.

In his first major discourse, the Lord Jesus Christ powerfully called his people to be both "the salt of the earth" and "the light of the world" (Matt. 5:13–14). Salt is an Old Testament image of preservation,[11] enhancing,[12] and purifying.[13] By declaring his followers to be salt, the Lord is calling us to preserve, enhance, and purify human life and culture. Light

---

[11] Salt was used in sacrifices to signify the permanence of God's covenant in that salt was an ancient preservative that hinders corruption: "All the offerings of the holy gifts, which the sons of Israel offer to the LORD, I have given to you and your sons and your daughters with you, as a perpetual allotment. It is an everlasting covenant of salt before the LORD" (Num. 18:19; cp. Lev. 2:13; 2 Chron. 13:5; Eze. 43:24).

[12] Job 6:6: "Can something tasteless be eaten without salt?" Matt. 5:13b supports this: "if the salt has become tasteless, how can it be made salty again?"

[13] Salt was often used in the Old Testament as an emblem of purity. For instance, in 2 Kgs. 2:21 we read Elisha's action: "He went out to the spring of water and threw salt in it and said, 'Thus says the LORD, "I have purified these waters."'" See also: Exo. 30:35; Eze. 16:4.

dispels darkness (Gen. 1:2–3; Isa. 9:2; Luke 11:36; 2 Cor. 4:6; Eph. 5:8). So Jesus is here calling us to bring God's light into all areas of this sin darkened world. One important implication of this is that since God created us as social creatures (Gen. 2:18) and dominion-oriented beings (Gen. 1:26–27), and established civil government and appointed the civil ruler as his "minister" (Rom. 3:1–4), we must speak to the world regarding how man is to govern his society.

We effectively see this confirmed in the Lord's Great Commission. As we have just seen, on the basis of "all authority" the Lord also commissioned us to bring the "nations" (whole societies and cultures) of the world under our discipleship instruction (Matt. 28:18–19). We wield the sword of the word — not the sword of the world — in conquering the hearts and minds of men (2 Cor. 10:4). We must speak and act as Christians to exercise Christ's authority in the whole world — including the political order.

Paul has much to say about the universal implications of the Christian worldview. And he recognizes that he is serving as a Lord with "all authority in heaven and on earth." In one of his earliest letters, he deals with a debate that erupts between Jewish and Gentile Christians over the question of eating ceremonially unclean foods (1 Cor. 8–10). As he gets to the end of his argument, he closes it by bring a universal principle to bear on this specific matter (or any other!): "Whether, then, you eat or drink or *whatever* you do, do *all* to the glory of God" (1 Cor. 10:31).

In his statement Paul presents us with a universal obligation: he declares that *whatever* we do we must do *all* to God's glory. Since we live in a world that absolutely requires governmental order, politics is one of the "all" things to which we must seek to glorify God. Elsewhere he commands: "*Whatever* you do in word or deed, do all in the name of the Lord Jesus, giving thanks through Him to God the Father" (Col. 3:17). As Peter teaches: "in all things God [must] be glorified through Jesus Christ" (1 Pet. 4:11).

In the follow-up to 1 Corinthians, Paul makes an even more powerful assertion regarding the Christian's calling: "we are destroying speculations and every lofty thing raised up against the knowledge of God, and we are taking every thought captive to the obedience of Christ" (2 Cor. 10:5). Once again Paul recognizes that he is serving a universal Lord who possesses "all authority." And once again he brings that reality to bear upon the Christian's calling in the world.

Here he states that he is seeking to destroy "speculations and every lofty thing raised up against the knowledge of God," which would include political issues. *Every* speculation which resists God is a target for his employing the Christian worldview. This is the negative way of putting the matter; but he expresses it positively as well. He declares that he is "taking every thought captive to the obedience of Christ." Not *some* thoughts. Not inner-personal, private thoughts. Not Sunday-only thoughts. *Every* thought; that is, every thought in *any* area of life. Including the important political realm.

Paul also informs us that "All Scripture is inspired by God . . . so that the man of God may be adequate, equipped for every good work" (2 Tim. 3:16). This includes the many parts of the Bible that directly touch on social and political issues (see previous discussion). Here the apostle sees the *Scripture* as a tool for equipping us for "*every* good work" — not just evangelistic work.

In fact, Paul sees a direct application of "the glorious gospel" and "sound teaching" itself to judicial-political issues covered in God's law:

> "But we know that the Law is good, if one uses it lawfully, realizing the fact that law is not made for a righteous person, but for those who are lawless and rebellious, for the ungodly and sinners, for the unholy and profane, for those who kill their fathers or mothers, for murderers and immoral men and homosexuals and kidnappers and liars and perjurers, and whatever else is contrary to sound teaching, according to the glorious gospel of the blessed God, with which I have been entrusted." (1 Tim. 1:8–11)

How can Christians avoid politics if both the "gospel" and "sound teaching" speak to judicial-political issues?

Paul even commands Christians: "Do not participate in the unfruitful deeds of darkness, but instead even expose them" (Eph. 5:11). This does not allow us to withdraw from the influence around us; it obligates us to "expose them." The Christian voice must be heard in the political realm. After all, Jesus even tells the Roman procurator: "For this I have been born, and for this I have come into the world, to testify to the truth" (John 18:37b).

But finally, we must engage the political application of the Christian worldview for practical reasons in that:

**Our predicament demands it**

Although God did not intend such, the State has become the dominant institution in human society. Throughout history political rulers have succumbed to Adam and Eve's temptation to "be like God" (Gen. 3:5). We see this mentioned frequently in Scripture:

- The "king of Babylon" (Isa. 14:4) boasted: "I will ascend above the heights of the clouds; / I will make myself like the Most High" (Isa. 14:14)

- The "leader of Tyre" (Eze. 28:1) proud declared: "I am a god, / I sit in the seat of gods" (Eze. 28:2; cp. v. 6)

- The Roman emperor minted coins declaring himself to be divine. The denarius to which Jesus responded had the following inscription on it: "Caesar Augustus Tiberius, son of the Divine Augustus." When Jesus saw this coin he warned: "Render to Caesar the things that are Caesar's; and to God the things that are God's." (Matt. 22:21)

- When Herod Antipas gave an address while seated on the rostrum, the people cried out: "The voice of a god and not of a man!" But then, we read: "immediately an angel of the Lord struck him because he did not give God the glory, and he was eaten by worms and died." (Acts 12:22, 23)

- Paul speaks of "the man of lawlessness" who "opposes and exalts himself above every so-called god or object of worship, so that he takes his seat in the temple of God, displaying himself as being God." (2 Thess. 2:4)[14]

- John presents a ten-crowned king (Rev. 13:1) as a powerful "beast" who had a "throne and great authority" (Rev. 13:2). Then we read of his subjects: "they worshiped the beast, saying, 'Who is like the beast?'" (Rev. 13:3; cp. 13:12, 15; 14:9, 11; 16:2; 19:20; 20:4).

---

[14] This is probably referring to Nero Caesar.

With the State's monopoly on the power of the sword — only the state has the right to capital punishment (Rom. 13:1–4) — this political god-lust has created all sorts of woes for men.

In that man is sinful, the governments of fallen man easily lapse into sin. We see this in what is happening in our own American government. John Newby states what evangelical Christians see all around them: "Christianity is under attack on the political, educational and media fronts."[15] Because of the growing problem, we see more and more books warning of this, such as:

- Nigel Leaves, *Religion Under Attack* (2011)
- Brad O'Leary, *America's War on Christianity* (2010)
- Erwin Lutzer, *When a Nation Forgets God* (2010)
- Donald E. Wildmon, *Speechless: Silencing the Christians* (2009)
- Janet L. Folger, *The Criminalization of Christianity* (2005)
- Craig Ostein, *The ACLU vs. America: Exposing the Agenda to Redefine Moral Values* (2005)
- David Limbaugh, *Persecution: How Liberals Are Waging War Against Christianity* (2004)
- D. James Kennedy, *The Gates of Hell Shall Not Prevail: The Attack on Christianity and What You Need To Know To Combat It* (1997)

Our current political circumstances are foreboding. Our faith is under attack. What are Christians to do? Can we withdraw ourselves from politics when our Christian faith is under such relentless assault and our religious freedoms are quickly eroding? Surely not.

God hates unrighteousness in any realm, but in the political sphere wickedness is especially reprehensible for it "devises mischief by decree" (Psa. 94:20b). Therefore, Christians must recognize the ultimate authority of Christ (Matt. 28:18) and bow to him as Lord. We *must* "expose the works of darkness" (Eph. 5:11) wherever those works are found — especially in politics where our liberties are threatened. Oftentimes we will find ourselves at odds with certain governmental policies because of our commitment to Christ. Like the apostles of old we must speak out politically, for "we must obey God rather than men" (Acts 5:29).

---

[15] http://www.newswithviews.com/guest_opinion/guest38.htm

Though America was founded as a basically Christian nation (see ch. 2), our nation has now become a secular state that is increasingly antagonistic to Christianity. We see a relentless erosion of our Christian freedoms and a suppression of our religious heritage in society and government. We cannot stand idly by and watch this national decline — especially since we still have the right to speak out and to seek political change. We can look into the world round about us and see how nations suppress the Christian faith by force of law, as in North Korea, Saudi Arabia, Iran, and other nations.

Christians must seek to impact our non-Christian culture, for Paul commands: "work out your salvation with fear and trembling, for it is God who is at work in you, both to will and to work for His good pleasure" (Phil. 2:12–13). He is not saying we are to "work *for* our salvation" for he later states his own hope in this very epistle: that "I may be found in Him, *not* having a righteousness of *my own* which is from he Law, but that which is through faith in Christ, righteousness which comes from God on the basis of faith" (Phil. 3:9). For Paul guilty sinners can *never* merit God's favor (Rom. 4:1–5; 11:6; Gal. 2:16; Eph. 2:8–9; 2 Tim. 1:9). Rather in Philippians 2:12–13 he means that the salvation we possess must be "worked out" into every area of our lives. This would include the political sphere which influences our lives every day — as we live under laws, pay taxes, and so forth. We *must* be "the salt of the earth" and "the light of the world" (Matt. 5:13, 14).

## Conclusion

Our Christian faith is holistic: it involves an entire world-and-life outlook. In this chapter I have defined and explained the Christian worldview in general, and have applied it to the political sphere in particular. I argued that the Bible does clearly establish a Christian worldview. And since it does create a distinctively Christian understanding of and approach to life, it must necessarily involve one of the biggest influences on our lives: politics.

Evangelical theologian Carl F. H. Henry wisely observed that if:

"we abandon the sociopolitical realm to its own devices, we shall fortify the misimpression that the public order falls wholly outside the command and will of God, that Christianity deals with private concerns only;

and we shall conceal the fact that government exists by God's will as His servant for the sake of justice and order."[16]

Historian Alvin Schmidt has amply documented how Christianity has long influenced government policies for the good.[17] He shows how Christians were responsible for outlawing child exposure (child abandonment to the elements), abortion, gladiatorial blood-baths, torture, burning alive of widows in India, abolishing slavery, and much, much more. Without a Christian worldview and a witness to politics, these moral, social, and political changes would not have been possible.

Too few Christians understand the notion of a worldview. And even fewer actually engage in a worldview analysis of the issues around us. But if our faith is to survive and prosper in America, we must begin thinking and acting in terms of biblically-framed outlook on all of life, including politics. In fact, this problem of deficient worldview thinking is largely to blame for the demise of the Christian faith in our nation. If Christians do not more earnestly engage the political process and speak out on moral and political issues, they will be defaulting to the non-Christians (see ch. 3 below for a sampling of the immoral influences of anti-Christian legislation and jurisprudence).

---

[16] Carl F. H. Henry, *Twilight of a Great Civilization* (Westchester, Ill.: Crossway, 1988), 20.

[17] Alvin Schmidt, *How Christianity Changed the World* (Grand Rapids: Zondervan, 2004).

## Chapter 2

# AMERICAN HISTORY

"Blessed is the nation whose God is the LORD."
(Psa. 33:12a)

## Introduction

Chapter 1 of our study of the Christian worldview showed that politics should be important to Christians, not as a means of imposing our will on others, but as a part of a full-orbed Christian witness. Unfortunately, worldview-thinking among Christians has greatly declined in our day. This may well explain *why* we are currently in such a bad political situation in America. Simply put: Christians do not *think* biblically, therefore they do not *act* biblically in the wider social world. And this realization should prompt us to re-engage the political sphere. After all, Irish statesman Edmund Burke (1729–97) put the matter well when he famously stated: "All that is necessary for the triumph of evil is that good men do nothing."

Most Christians know that America is in a serious state of moral, social, cultural, and political decline. What we need to understand is that if our nation has declined, this implies that it has declined from a better situation. And such is certainly the case. As Christians we recognize the significance of a nation's religious faith to its well-being, for God's word states: "Blessed is the nation whose God is the LORD" (Psa. 33:12a). Indeed, it warns: "The wicked will return to Sheol, / Even all the nations who forget God" (Psa. 9:17).

Although the religious situation in America has certainly never been perfect, it has been much better. We can look back on a national history that was greatly influenced, strengthened, and blessed by the Christian faith. Christian social critic Os Guinness well notes that "while America has never officially been a 'Christian Republic,' for much of its history the Christian faith has been a leading contribution to its unofficial civil religion."[1] In fact, in an 1892 U. S. Supreme Court decision Justice David J. Brewer (1837–1910) stated that:

> "If we pass beyond these matters to a view of American life as expressed by its laws, its business, its customs and its society, we find everywhere a clear recognition of the same truth . . . this is a Christian nation."[2]

Unfortunately, our national situation is so different now and declining so much more rapidly today. For instance, in political speeches Barack Obama (while a senator and then later the president) has repeatedly sought to detach America from its Christian heritage. On June 28, 2006 he stated: "Whatever we once were, we are no longer a Christian nation." He repeated this in an email to CBN's David Brody in 2007. After he became president and while speaking at a press conference in Turkey on May 7, 2009, he stated casually: "we do not consider ourselves a Christian nation."[3]

Removing Christianity from America is dangerous because it leaves a hole in the nation's historical foundation and emptiness in our moral soul. The political world is much like the natural world in an important respect: nature abhors a vacuum. When a vacuum is created, dirt is sucked in. This vacuum-principle works fine in cleaning dirty carpets, but is disastrous when accidentally exiting an orbiting spacecraft or intentionally ejecting a national heritage.

When political statements remove Christianity from our national history, secular humanism is sucked in as it replacement. Even a theologian as liberal as Harvey Cox of Harvard University notes that secular humanism is "a new closed worldview which functions very much like a new religion . . . where it pretends not to be a world view but nonetheless seeks to impose its ideology through the organs of the state."[4] He then warns that it "has no tolerance and is opposed to other religions; it

---

[1] Os Guinness, *American Hour: A Time of Reckoning and the Once and Future Role of Faith* (New York: Simon & Schuster, 1993), 225.

[2] U. S. Supreme Court, *Church of the Holy Trinity v. United States*, 1892.

[3] http://www.msnbc.msn.com/id/30065504/ns/world_news-europe /t/obama -tells-turkey-us-not-war-islam/

[4] Harvey Cox, *The Secular City: Secularization and urbanization in Theological Perspective*, rev. ed. (New York: Macmillan, 1965, 1966), 18.

actively rejects, excludes and attempts to eliminate traditional theism from meaningful participation in the American culture."

Thus, the problem in American politics is never the question of religion or no religion. Rather it is the question of *which* religion. To remove Christian theism is to adopt secular humanism, which itself is a religious orientation.[5] To forbid the sacred is to endorse the secular.

If we are ever to have a renewed confidence in America's future, we need to have a rejuvenated commitment to America's past. This will require the Christian's political participation, beginning with studying the issues and voting on the candidates according to a Christian worldview analysis. One essential ingredient in motivating Christians to this end is to encourage them to realize that Christianity *can* have a positive influence on government in the future — because it *has* had a significant impact on it in the past.

In this chapter I will focus on the enormous influence of Christianity on our nation's history. Though we have much material available on the topic, and though large books have been written on it,[6] I will briefly summarize it under three headings:

Our Colonial Foundation
Our Legal History
Our Recent Past
So let's get started with:

### Our Colonial Foundation

A great many of the earliest and most important legal documents associated with the settling and founding of America specifically declare a commitment to the Christian faith. Though such legal declarations

---

[5] In the 1961 Supreme Court decision Torasco vs. Watkins, Justice Hugo Black wrote: "Among the religions in this country which do not teach what would generally be considered a belief in the existence of God are Buddhism, Taoism, Ethical Culture, Secular Humanism, and others." http://scholar.google.com/scholar_case?case=17484916405561277413&hl=en&as_sdt=2&as_vis=1&oi=scholarr

[6] Two invaluable resources in this regard are: Benjamin Franklin Morris (1810 –1867), *The Christian Life and Character of the Civil Institutions of the United States* (Powder Springs, Geo.: American Vision, 2007 [rep. 1864]) and Gary DeMar's three-volume study, *God and Government* (updated edition: Powder Springs, Geo.: American Vision, 2001).

would create a furor today, they were entirely commonplace, virtually instinctive, and generally expected long ago. For some of these I will provide fuller statements; for others just a few snippets. These few samples should motivate us today to see that the Christian faith can have a strong and positive influence in political endeavors.

## First Charter of Virginia (April 10, 1606)

"We, greatly commending and graciously accepting of their Desires for the Furtherance of so noble a Work, which may, by the Providence of Almighty God, hereafter tend to the Glory of His Divine Majesty, in propagating of Christian Religion to such People, as yet live in Darkness and miserable Ignorance of the true Knowledge and Worship of God, and may in time bring the Infidels and Savages, living in those Parts, to human Civility, and to a settled and quiet Government."

## Second Charter of Virginia (May 23, 1609)

"Because the principal Effect which we can expect or desire of this Action is the Conversion and reduction of the people in those parts unto the true worship of God and the Christian Religion."

## Mayflower Compact (November 11,1620)

"In ye name of God, Amen. We whose names are underwritten,… having undertaken, for ye glorie of God, and advancemente of ye Christian faith, and honour of our king, & countrie, a voyage to plant ye first colonie in ye Northerne parts of Virginia, doe by these presents solemnly & mutually in ye presence of God, and one of another, covenant & combine our selves togeather into a civill body politick, for our better ordering & preservation & furtherance of ye ends aforesaid; and by vertue hearof to enacte, constitute, and frame such just & equall lawes, ordinances, acts, constitutions & offices, from time to time, as shall be thought most meete & convenient for ye generall good of ye Colonie, unto which we promise all due submission and obedience.

"In witness wherof we have hereunder subscribed our names at Cap-Codd ye 11. of November, in ye year of ye raigne of our soveraigne lord, King James, of England, France, & Ireland ye eighteenth, and by Scotland ye fiftie fourth, Ano: Dom. 1620."

## First Charter of Massachusetts (March 4, 1629)

"For the directing, ruling, and disposeing of all other Matters and Things, whereby our said People... maie be soe religiously, peaceable, and civilly governed, as their good life and orderlie Conversation, maie wynn and incite the Natives of the Country to the Knowledg and Obedience of the onlie true God and Savior of Mankinde, and the Christian Fayth, which, in our Royall Intention, and the Adventurers free profession, is the principall Ende of this Plantation."

## Charter of Carolina (March 24, 1663)

"Being excited with a laudable and pious zeal for the propagation of the Christian faith... [they] have humbly besought leave of us... to transport and make an ample colony... unto a certain country... in the parts of America not yet cultivated or planted, and only inhabited by some barbarous people, who have no knowledge of Almighty God."

## Charter of Rhode Island and Providence Plantations (July 8, 1663)

"We submit our persons, lives, and estates unto our Lord Jesus Christ, the King of kings and Lord of lords and to all those perfect and most absolute laws of His given us in His Holy Word."

"That they, pursueing, with peaceable and loyall mindes, sober, serious and religious intentions, of godlie edifieing themselves, and one another, in the holie Christian ffaith and worshipp... together with the gaineing over and conversione of the poore ignorant Indian natives... a most flourishing civill state may stand and best bee maintained... grounded upon gospell principles."

## Charter of Pennsylvania (March 4, 1681)

"To reduce the savage natives by gentle and just manners to the Love of Civil Societe and Christian Religion."

### Our Legal History

With the colonies receiving charters containing express declarations of fidelity to the Christian faith, our foundations as a nation were firmly laid. As the colonies were more fully settled they began to establish law orders and constitutions continuing in this tradition.

Fundamental Orders (Constitution) of Connecticut (January 14, 1639) (the first constitution written in America)

> "Forasmuch as it has pleased the Almighty God by the wise disposition of His divine providence so to order and dispose of things that we the inhabitants and residents of Windsor, Hartford and Wethersfield and now cohabiting and dwelling in and upon the River Connecticut and the lands thereunto adjoining; and well knowing when a people are gathered together the Word of God requires, that to meinteine the peace and union of such a people, there should bee an orderly and decent government established according to God, to order and dispose of the affairs of all the people at all seasons as occasion shall require; do therefore associate and conjoin ourselves to be as one public State or Commonwealth, and do, for ourselves and our successors and such as shall be adjoined to us at any time hereafter, enter into Combination and Confederation together, to meinteine and presearve the libberty and purity of the Gospell of our Lord Jesus which we now professe... Which, according to the truth of the said Gospell, is now practised amongst us; as allso, in our civill affaires to be guided and governed according to such laws, rules, orders, and decrees."

## Articles of the Constitution of Connecticut (January 14, 1639)

> "Article I. That the Scriptures hold forth a perfect rule for the direction and government of all men in all duties which they are to perform to God and men, as well in families and commonwealths as in matters of the church.

> "Article II. That as in matters which concern the gathering and ordering of a church, so likewise in all public offices which concern civil order, -- as the choice of magistrates and officers, making and repealing laws, dividing allotments of inheritance, and all things of like nature, — they would all be governed by those rules which the Scripture held forth to them.

> "Article III. That all those who had desired to be received free planters had settled in the plantation with a purpose, resolution, and desire that they might be admitted into church fellowship according to Christ.

> "Article IV. That all the free planters held themselves bound to establish such civil order as might best conduce to the securing of the purity and peace of the ordinance to themselves, and their posterity according to God."

## Constitution of the New England Confederation (May 19, 1643)

"The Articles of Confederation between the plantations under the government of Massachusetts, the plantations under the government of New Plymouth, the plantations under the government of Connecticut, and the government of New Haven with the plantations in combination therewith:

"Whereas we all came to these parts of America with the same end and aim, namely, to advance the Kingdome of our Lord Jesus Christ, and to injoy the liberties of the Gospell thereof with purities and peace, and for preserving and propagating the truth and liberties of the gospell."

## Fundamental Constitutions of Pennsylvania (April 25, 1682)

"Considering that it is impossible that any People or Government should ever prosper, where men render not unto God, that which is God's, as well as to Caesar, that which is Caesar's; and also perceiving that disorders and Mischiefs that attend those places where force is used in matters of faith and worship, and seriously reflecting upon the tenure of the new and Spiritual Government, and that both Christ did not use force and that he did expressly forbid it in his holy Religion, as also that the Testimony of his blessed Messengers was, that the weapons of the Christian warfare were not Carnall but Spiritual...

"Therefore, in reverence to God the Father of lights and spirits, the Author as well as object of all divine knowledge, faith and worship, I do hereby declare for me and myn and establish it for the first fundamental of the Government of my Country; that every Person that does or shall reside therein shall have and enjoy the Free Possession of his or her faith and exercise of worship towards God; in such way and manner as every Person shall in Conscience believe is most acceptable to God and so long as every such Person useth not this Christian liberty to Licentiousness, that is to say to speak loosely and prophainly of God, Christ or Religion, or to Committ any evil in their Conversation [lifestyle], he or she shall be protected in the enjoyment of the aforesaid Christian liberty by the civill Magistrate...."

## Great Law of Pennsylvania (April 25, 1682)

"Whereas the glory of Almighty God and the good of mankind is the reason and the end of government, and, therefore government itself is a venerable ordinance of God... [there shall be established] laws as shall best preserve true Christian and civil liberty, in opposition to all unchristian, licentious, and unjust practices, whereby God may have his due, and Caesar his due, and the people their due, from tyranny and oppression."

## Charter of Privileges of Pennsylvania (October 28, 1701)

"Almighty God being the only Lord of Conscience... and Author as well as object of all Divine Knowledge, faith and worship, who only doth enlighten the minds and persuade and convince the understandings of people, I do hereby grant and declare: that no person or persons, inhabiting in this province or territory who shall confess and acknowledge our Almighty God and Creator, Upholder and Ruler of the world; and profess him or themselves obliged to live quietly under civil government, shall in any case molested or prejudiced in his or her person or estate...

"And that all persons who also profess to believe in Jesus Christ, the Savior of the World, shall be capable to serve this government in any capacity, both legislatively or executively.

"No people can be truly happy, though under the greatest enjoyment of civil liberties, if abridged of... their religious profession and worship...."

## Constitution of the State of Maryland (August 14, 1776)

"Article XXXV. That no other test or qualification ought to be required, on admission to any office of trust or profit, than such oath of support and fidelity to this State and such oath of office, as shall be directed by this Convention, or the Legislature of this State, and a declaration of a belief in the Christian religion;

"That, as it is the duty of every man to worship God is such a manner as he thinks most acceptable to him; all persons professing the Christian religion, are equally entitled to protection in their religious liberty;

"Wherefore no person ought by any law to be molested... on account of his religious practice; unless, under the color of religion, any man shall disturb the good order, peace or safety of the State, or shall infringe the laws of morality... yet the Legislature may, in their discretion, lay a general and equal tax, for the support of the Christian religion."

## The Constitution of the State of Delaware (September 10, 1776)

"ART. 22. Every person who shall be chosen a member of either house, or appointed to any office or place of trust, before taking his seat, or entering upon the execution of his office, shall take the following oath, or affirmation, if conscientiously scrupulous of taking an oath, to wit:

"'I, A B. will bear true allegiance to the Delaware State, submit to its constitution and laws, and do no act wittingly whereby the freedom thereof may be prejudiced.'

And also make and subscribe the following declaration, to wit:

"'I, A B. do profess faith in God the Father, and in Jesus Christ His only Son, and in the Holy Ghost, one God, blessed for evermore; and I do acknowledge the holy scriptures of the Old and New Testament to be given by divine inspiration.'"

## Constitution of the State of North Carolina (December 18, 1776)

"Article XXXII. That no person who shall deny the being of God, or the truth of the Protestant religion, or the divine authority of the Old or New Testaments, or who shall hold religious principles incompatible with the freedom and safety of the State, shall be capable of holding any office or place of trust or profit in the civil department within this State."

## Constitution of the State of Vermont (July 8, 1777)

"Frame of Government, Section 9. And each member [of the Legislature], before he takes his seat, shall make and subscribe the following declaration, viz: 'I do believe in one God, the Creator and Governor of the universe, the rewarder of the good and punisher of the wicked. And I do acknowledge the Scripture of the Old and New Testament to be given by divine inspiration, and own and profess the [Christian] religion. And no further or other religious test shall ever, hereafter, be required of any civil officer or magistrate in this State.'"

## Constitution of the State of South Carolina (March 19, 1778)

"Article XXXVIII. That all persons and religious societies who acknowledge that there is one God, and a future state of rewards and punishments, and that God is publicly to be worshipped, shall be freely tolerated... That all denominations of Christian[s]... in this State, demeaning themselves peaceably and faithfully, shall enjoy equal religious and civil privileges."

## The Constitution of the State of Massachusetts (June 15, 1780)

"Part the First. Art. III. As the happiness of a people and the good order and preservation of civil government essentially depend upon piety, religion, and morality, and as these cannot be generally diffused through a community but by the institution of the public worship of God and of the public instructions in piety, religion, and morality: Therefore, To promote their happiness and to secure the good order and preservation of their government, the people of this commonwealth have a right to invest their legislature with power to authorize and require, and the legislature shall, from time to time, authorize and require, the several towns, parishes, precincts, and other bodies-politic or religious societies to make suitable provision, at their own expense, for the institution of the public worship of God and for the support and maintenance of public Protestant teachers of piety, religion, and morality in all cases where such provision shall not be made voluntarily.

"Chapter 2. Art. II. The governor shall be chosen annually; and no person shall be eligible to this office, unless, at the time of his election, he shall have been an inhabitant of this commonwealth for seven years next preceding; and unless he shall, at the same time, be seized, in his own right, of a freehold, within the commonwealth, of the value of one thousand pounds; and unless he shall declare himself to be of the Christian religion.

"Chapter 5. Art. I. Whereas our wise and pious ancestors, so early as the year [1636], laid the foundation of Harvard College, in which university many persons of great prominence have, by the blessing of God, been initiated in those arts and sciences which qualified them for the public employments, both in church and State; and whereas the encouragement of arts and sciences, and all good literature, tends to the honor of God, the advantage of the Christian religion, and the great benefit of this and the other United States of America.

"Chapter 6. Art. I. Any person chosen governor, lieutenant-governor, councillor, senator, or representative, and accepting the trust, shall, before he proceed to execute the duties of his place or office, make and subscribe the following declaration, viz:

"'I, A.B., do declare that I believe the Christian religion, and have a firm persuasion of its truth; and that I am seized and possessed, in my own right, of the property required by the constitution, as one qualification for the office or place to which I am elected.'

## Constitution of the State of New Hampshire (June 2, 1784)

"VI. As morality and piety, rightly grounded on evangelical principles, will give the best and greatest security to government, and will lay in the hearts of men the strongest obligations to due subjection; and as the knowledge of these, is most likely to be propagated through a society by the institution of the public worship of the DEITY, and of public instruction in morality and religion; therefore, to promote those important purposes, the people of this state have a right to impower, and do hereby fully impower the legislature to authorize from time to time, the several towns, parishes, bodies corporate, or religious societies within this state, to make adequate provision at their own expence, for the support and maintenance of public protestant teachers of piety, religion and morality."

## Constitution of the State of Tennessee (February 6, 1796)

"Article VIII, Section II. No person who denies the being of God, or a future state of rewards and punishments, shall hold any office in the civil department of this State."

## The People v. Ruggles, (Justice James Kent, U.S. Supreme Court, 1811)

"The people of this State, in common with the people of this country, profess the general doctrines of Christianity, as the rule of their faith and practice . . . . We are a Christian people, and the morality of the country is deeply engrafted upon Christianity, and not upon the doctrines of worship of those impostors [other religions] . . . . Christianity in its enlarged sense, as a religion revealed and taught in the Bible, is part and parcel of the law of the land. . . . We are a Christian people, and the morality of this country is deeply engrafted upon Christianity, and not upon the doctrines or worship of these impostors."

Chief Justice John Marshall, in a letter to Jasper Adams (May 9, 1833[7])

> "The American population is entirely Christian, and with us Christianity and Religion are identified. It would be strange indeed, if with such a people, our institutions did not presuppose Christianity, and did not often refer to it, and exhibit relations with it."

Joseph Story (U. S. Supreme Court; Founder Harvard Law School) (1833)

> "At the time of the adoption of the Constitution, the general, if not the universal, sentiment in America was, that Christianity ought to receive encouragement from the State so far as was not incompatible with the private rights of conscience and the freedom of religious worship."[8]

Richmond v. Moore, 1883 (Illinois Supreme Court):

> "Our laws and our institutions must necessarily be based upon and embody the teachings of the Redeemer of mankind. It is impossible that it should be otherwise. In this sense and to this extent, our civilizations and our institutions are emphatically Christian."[9]

"Holy Trinity Church v. the United States" (U. S. Supreme Court, February 29, 1892[10])

(Note: this Supreme Court decision cites a large body of legal statements from American history and makes the following declarations on this basis.)

> "But, beyond all these matters, no purpose of action against religion can be imputed to any legislation, state or national, because this is a reli-

---

[7] http://candst.tripod.com/jaspltrs.htm

[8] Joseph Story, *Commentaries on the Constitution of the United States: With a Preliminary Review of the Constitutional History of the Colonies and States, Before the Adoption of the Constitution* (Cambridge: Brown, Shattuck, 1833), 3:726.

[9] Cited in Isaac Amada Cornelison, *The Relation of Religion to Civil Government in the United States of America: A State Without a Church, but Not Without a Religion* (New York: Putnams, 1923), 134.

[10] The Supreme Court of the United States, Holy Trinity Church V. the United States 143 u.s. 457, 12 s.ct. 511, 36 l.ed. 226, February 29, 1892.

gious people. This is historically true. From the discovery of this continent to the present hour, there is a single voice making this affirmation.

. . .

"There is no dissonance in these declarations. There is a universal language pervading them all, having one meaning. They affirm and reaffirm that this is a religious nation. These are not individual sayings, declarations of private persons. They are organic utterances. They speak the voice of the entire people.

. . .

"If we pass beyond these matters to a view of American life, as expressed by its laws, its business, its customs, and its society, we find everywhere a clear recognition of the same truth. Among other matters note the following: The form of oath universally prevailing, concluding with an appeal to the Almighty; the custom of opening sessions of all deliberative bodies and most conventions with prayer; the prefatory words of all wills, "In the name of God, amen;" the laws respecting the observance of the Sabbath, with the general cessation of all secular business, and the closing of courts, legislatures, and other similar public assemblies on that day; the churches and church organizations which abound in every city, town, and hamlet; the multitude of charitable organizations existing everywhere under Christian auspices; the gigantic missionary associations, with general support, and aiming to establish Christian missions in every quarter of the globe. These and many other matters which might be noticed, add a volume of unofficial declarations to the mass of organic utterances that this is a Christian nation."

## U.S. vs. Macintosh, 1931 (Justice George Sutherland, U.S. Supreme Court)

"We are a Christian people... and acknowledge with reverence the duty of obedience to the will of God."[11]

## Our National Anthem

On March 3, 1931, the U. S. Congress adopted "The Star Spangled Banner" as our National Anthem. The fourth verse is of our national anthem reads:

"O! thus be it ever when free men shall stand
Between their loved home and the war's desolation;

---

[11] US vs. Macintosh. 283 US 605.

Blest with vict'ry and peace, may the heav'n-rescued land
Praise the Pow'r that hath made and preserv'd us a nation!

"Then conquer we must, when our cause it is just;
And this be our motto, "In God is our trust!"
And the star spangled banner in triumph shall wave
O'er the land of the free and the home of the brave!"[12]

Our National Motto

By Joint Resolution on July 20, 1956, the U.S. Congress as America's national motto:

"In God We Trust"

Thus, we can see why that early on in our national history (1840) Alexis de Tocqueville could write:

"There is no country in the world where the Christian religion retains a greater influence over the souls of men than in America; and there can be no greater proof of its utility, and of its conformity to human nature, than that its influence is most powerfully felt over the most enlightened and free nation on the earth."[13]

## Conclusion

This short list of overtly religious and distinctly Christian statements should dispel the notion that America is not in any sense a Christian nation. These should, therefore, inspire the recognition that America could return to a Christian conviction. In fact, two law professors at the University of Houston, Donald S. Lutz and Charles S. Hyneman, surveyed 916 printed political documents containing more than 2000 words from 1760–1805. They noted that the most frequently cited source was the Bible, which was specifically cited 34% of the time.[14]

––––––––––––––––––––

[12] 46 Stat. 1508, codified at 36 U.S.C. § 301.

[13] Alexis de Tocqueville, *Democracy in America* (New York, N.Y.: Vintage Classics, 1990), 303.

[14] Donald S. Lutz, "The Relative Influence of European Writers on Late Eighteenth-Century American Political Thought," *American Political Science Review*, 78:1 (1984), 189–97.

Even as we state this, though, we must understand that the Christian worldview rooted in Scripture does establish an *institutional* separation of church and state, even while it discourages a separation of God from government. As I close out this chapter, I must explain this important matter.

When we read God's Law in the Old Testament, we find that Israel's civil head and the ecclesiastical head were separate and distinct offices. Moses was the civil head of Israel upon forming the people as a nation (Exo. 18:13); Aaron was the head of the church. Aaron, not Moses, was the one who was "to minister as a priest to Me," says the Lord (Exo. 18:1; 19:7–8); Aaron was the "anointed priest" (Lev. 4:3). In fact, the ancient priesthood became known as "the sons of Aaron" (Lev. 1:7; 3:13; Num. 3:2; Josh. 21:4; etc.), not "the sons of Moses."

In the appointment of Moses and Aaron to their respective callings we must note a distinction between the civil leader and the ecclesiastical leader. Though Melchizedek embodied *both* offices (Gen. 14:18), he lived *before* Israel was formed as a nation and did not serve as a model for national leadership in that regard.

We also discover that the line of the kings of Israel sprang for a different source than that of the priests. Judah was promised the line of kingship in Genesis 49:10. From his loins sprang both David and David's greater son, Christ (Matt. 1:1–2, 6; Rev. 5:5). As the writers of Hebrews puts it: "For it is evident that our Lord was descended from Judah, a tribe with reference to which Moses spoke nothing concerning priests" (Heb. 7:14).

In keeping with this distinction between the officers of church and state, we discover that Israel kept the king's palace distinct from the priest's temple: "Now Solomon decided to build a house for the name of the Lord, and a royal palace for himself" (2 Chron. 2:1; cp. 7:11; 9:11; 28:21).

The civil and ecclesiastical functions were clearly distinguished: "Amariah the chief priest will be over you in all that pertains to the Lord; and Zebadiah the son of Ishmael, the ruler of the house of Judah, in all that pertains to the king" (2 Chron. 19:11a).

Despite the authority of the king in Israel, not even he was allowed to enter the holy of holies. "Into the second only the high priest enters, once a year, not without taking blood, which he offers for himself and for the sins of the people committed in ignorance" (Heb. 9:7; cf. Lev. 16).

Indeed, kings were strictly forbidden to take up priestly functions. Samuel scathingly rebuked Saul for offering a burnt-offering (1 Sam. 13:11). Uzziah was denounced by Azariah the priest and turned leprous for his presumption in this regard (2 Chron. 26:16–19). Thus, though in Israel church and state closely *cooperated*, they were not inextricably *united*.

## Chapter 3
# MORAL VALUES

"Righteousness exalts a nation, / But sin is a disgrace to any people."
(Prov. 14:34)

### Introduction
This book has been written out of an intense concern regarding the sad state of America's political situation. Our nation's accelerating political decline is being drawn along in the turbulent downdraft of its increasing moral tailspin.

My previous chapter emphasized the strong Christian influence on our culture and our nation in the past, including its political institutions. It also noted the recent political tendency to downgrade, denigrate, and dismiss our religious foundations and Christian heritage. This is not a mere academic problem of secondary interest. Rather, we see in this the dominos of cultural collapse: religious defection leads to moral degeneration which results in political decline.

I will show in this chapter that by the very nature of the case politics involves moral issues. Consequently, moral standards are important for politics. Let us begin by briefly considering:

### Our Current Predicament
In 1993 William J. Bennett, former education secretary for the federal government, wrote an Op-ed piece in the *Wall Street Journal* which has been widely cited. In this article he lamented: "What is shocking is just how precipitously American life has declined in the past 30 years."[1] Many Christian social critics have sounded the alarm regarding how rapidly morality has declined in America. Many of these recognize our moral problem as linked with our religious defection.

In their book *Personal Faith, Public Policy*, Harry Jackson and Tony Perkins relate this to increased secularism. They note that by the mid-

---

[1] William J. Bennett, "Quantifying America's Decline," *Wall Street Journal* (March 15, 1993). You may read this article at: http://www.columbia.edu /cu/ augustine/arch/usadecline.html

20th century "America had undergone an ugly and extreme transformation at the hands of radical secularists."[2]

Pete Fisher agrees when he notes:

> "Then the massive thrust of television and theaters that taught these same people that sex, and alternative lifestyles, marital infidelity, and divorce are all to be accepted as normal. The violence from Hollywood has also inundated the minds of our society, and has taken root as well. And even further, is the Liberal PC movement that takes into regard many of these lifestyles and embraces them as acceptable, all the while bashing Christianity and its value system. We have allowed in this nation to have the Bible, and mention of Christian values taken from society and have allowed all these other immoral and destructive behaviors and lifestyles to become seen as normal."[3]

Fox News commentator Bill O'Reilly follows suit:

> "The belief that America is degenerating on a moral level is shared by both Republicans and Democrats. According to a new Gallup poll, 82 percent of Republicans and 78 percent of Democrats say that moral values in the U.S.A. are only fair or downright poor. 40 years ago, only 33 percent of Americans felt that way.
> So what's happened? First, secular forces have destroyed any rendering of Judeo-Christian philosophy in the public school system. . . ."[4]

This moral decline is significant in that "an established morality is as necessary as good government to the welfare of society. Societies disintegrate from within more frequently than they are broken up by external pressures."[5] We must understand that wide-scale social immorality leads to a wholesale cultural implosion. "Righteousness exalts a nation, / But sin is a disgrace to any people" (Prov. 14:34).

---

[2] Harry R. Jackson, Jr. and Tony Perkins, *Personal Faith, Public Policy* (Lake Mary, Fla: FrontLine, 2008), 2.

[3] Pete Fisher, "The Decline of Morality in our Society," Renew America website (Oct. 5, 2005). http://www.renewamerica.com/columns/fisher/051005

[4] Bill O'Reilly, "The Decline of Morality in America," FoxNews (May 27, 2004). http://www.foxnews.com/story/0,2933,121064,00.html

[5] Patrick Devlin in Ronald Dworkin, Taking Rights Seriously (Cambridge, Mass.: Harvard University Press, 1977), 76-77. Devlin (1905–92) was a prominent British judge.

Regarding the role of the religious foundations to morality, General Douglas MacArthur well-stated in the middle of the last century:

> "In this day of gathering storms, as moral deterioration of political power spreads its growing infection, it is essential that every spiritual force be mobilized to defend and preserve the religious base upon which this nation is founded; for it has been that base which has been the motivating impulse to our moral and national growth. History fails to record a single precedent in which nations subject to moral decay have not passed into political and economic decline. There has been either a spiritual reawakening to overcome the moral lapse, or a progressive deterioration leading to ultimate national disaster."[6]

Joseph Stalin, the atheistic dictator of the Soviet Union, confirmed this observation when he stated: "America is like a healthy body and its resistance is threefold: its patriotism, its morality, and its spiritual life. If we can undermine these three areas, America will collapse from within."[7]

## Our Moral Foundation

Our nation needs to return to its Christian roots for a very important reason: "if the foundations are destroyed, / What can the righteous do?" (Psa. 11:3). Political rulers are important for insuring that we "may lead a tranquil and quiet life in all godliness and dignity" (1 Tim. 2:2). They should not be "a cause of fear for good behavior, but for evil" as they "they bear the sword" (Rom. 3:3–4). Therefore, they must function "for the punishment of evildoers and the praise of those who do right" (1 Pet. 2:14). But secularism cannot even affirm morality, much less protect and promote it, because the non-Christian system has no sure base for it. Let me explain this (too) briefly.

The secularists' *reality* is ultimately founded on nothing more than a gigantic explosion 13.5 billion years ago.[8] Thus, in the secularist's

---

[6] This is from a speech given to the Salvation Army on December 12, 1951. Gen. Douglas F. MacArthur, *A Soldier Speaks: Public Papers and Speeches of General of the Army Douglas MacArthur* (New York: Praeger, 1965), 285–286.

[7] Josef Stalin Quote on the *Liberty-Tree.ca* website. http://quotes. liberty -tree.ca/quote_blog/Josef.Stalin.Quote.CC49

[8] "The Big Bang Model is a broadly accepted theory for the origin and evolution of our universe. It postulates that 12 to 14 billion years ago, the portion of the universe we can see today was only a few millimeters across. It has since

worldview *knowledge* is rooted in irrationalism in that reality is rooted in chance (the impersonal flux of a random universe). As a result, *morality* is necessarily reduced to pure relativism and because of this can be nothing more than personal preference. In such a system there are no ultimate, universal, invariant, obligatory moral standards — indeed, there *can* be none. As a consequence, non-Christian thought can offer no rational justification for any moral behavior whatsoever. Nor can it logically condemn any moral action, even one as heinous as the Nazi Holocaust.

For the Christian, morality is founded upon the all-good, all-knowing, everywhere-present, all-powerful, eternally-existing, infinitely-personal, and self-revealing God of Scripture.[9] His will, which is rooted in his being and nature, and is revealed in Scripture is man's standard of morality (Rom. 7:12). Since God is all-knowing (Psa. 139:2–27; Prov. 15:3) and everywhere-present (1 Kgs. 8:27; Jer. 23:24), moral principles revealed in Scripture are always *relevant* to our situation. Since God is all-good (Psa. 119:137; Mark 10:18b) and eternal (Psa. 90:2; 102:12), his moral commands are always *binding* upon men.

Many resist the Christian's promotion of the Bible's moral standards in society and politics. They claim that you cannot impose morality. But all law — secular or sacred — is by the very nature of the case an imposing of morality. In fact, moral imposition by law is important and necessary: The framing of laws against rape and murder imposes a morality upon rapists and murderers.

Furthermore, we must recognize that all law is implicitly religious. This is because all law is rooted in morality, and morality is based on ideas of ultimacy and value. And ultimacy and value are religious (transcendental) concepts which are not derived in the laboratory or effected by mathematical formulas. It is precisely to this principle that George Washington spoke in his farewell address on September 19, 1796 when he said:

---

expanded from this hot dense state into the vast and much cooler cosmos we currently inhabit." From "Big Bang Cosmology," on the NASA website. http://map.gsfc.nasa.gov/universe/bb_theory.html

[9] The Christian worldview is the only rational system of thought and action. This is because of the impossibility of the contrary. That is, given our presupposition of the God of Scripture, we can give an account of reality and justify knowledge and morality. But given the non-Christian's presupposition of chance, they cannot account for reality, knowledge, and morality.

"And let us with caution indulge the supposition, that morality can be maintained without religion. Whatever may be conceded to the influence of refined education on minds of peculiar structure, reason, and experience both forbids us to expect that National morality can prevail in exclusion of religious principle."[10]

In this regard, famed historian Will Durant wrote: "There is no significant example in history, before our time, of a society successfully maintaining moral life without the aid of religion."[11]

For these reasons our social, cultural, and political circumstances *demand* a Christian witness and political engagement. We *must* be "the salt of the earth" and "the light of the world" if we are to obediently follow Christ — and to retrieve our culture from ruin as an inheritance to be passed on to our children.

## Our Political Lethargy

Sadly though, too many Christians deem Christian engagement in politics as unbiblical, unproductive, and even unsafe. In the early 1950's prominent radio evangelist J. Vernon McGee famously asked: "Do you polish brass on a sinking ship?" Best-selling author and televangelist Hal Lindsey has stated: "I don't like cliches but I've heard it said, 'God didn't send me to clean the fish bowl, he sent me to fish."[12] A current website updates these observations: "Who would go into a condemned building and start painting the walls and replacing broken windows? Who would stay on a sinking ship washing dirty dishes in the galley? That's what it is like to become entangled in this world and its politics."[13]

Even many influential scholars have discouraged Christian political action on similar grounds. After secular humanism came to a head in our culture, theologian and best-selling author John F. Walvoord provided Christians a comfort in their lethargy: "Perhaps Christians are not as concerned about social, political, and moral conditions in the world as they should be; but, on the other hand, it is not God's purpose in our present

---

[10] George Washington in William Jackson Johnstone, *George Washington, the Christian* (New York: Abingdon, 1919), 223.

[11] Will Durant and Ariel Durant, T*he Lessons of History* Selection 6: 1968: Chapter VI; Morals and History; Page 51

[12] "The Great Cosmic Countdown," *Eternity* (Jan., 1977): 21.

[13] Carl Knott, "The Christian and Politics," http://www.lifehouse. org /tracts/ thechristianandpolitics.htm

age to have social justice or to have all the ills and problems of life removed now."[14] He further noted that "Christians have no immediate solution to the problems of our day."[15]

More recently theologian Wayne House has warned Christians that any "attempt to establish long-term change in institutions will only result in the leaven of humanism permeating Christianity."[16] Influential best-selling author John F. MacArthur, agrees: "'Reclaiming' the culture is a pointless, futile exercise. I am convinced we are living in a post-Christian society—a civilization that exists under God's judgment."[17]

This is tragic in and of itself, in that it refuses to heed Christ's world-impacting call to "disciple the nations" (Matt. 28:19) under his claim of "all [not *some!*] authority in heaven and on earth" (Matt. 28:18). As we saw earlier, this includes even political authority (Eph. 1:21; Phil. 2:9; Rev. 19:16) because it encompasses *all* authority — even "on *earth.*"

These sentiments are also unaware of important realities of religious history. Theologian R. J. Rushdoony reminds us of the words of church historian Kenneth S. Latourette, noting that "the church has, he declares, advanced precisely in the areas and periods of cultural collapse and hence from the beginning established itself in the culturally dying Roman Empire."[18] What if the first Christians had refused to promote Christ's holistic call? Christianity would have quickly faded into oblivion, hiding its light under a basket (Matt. 5:15) while refusing to "expose the works of darkness" (Eph. 5:11). It would have been "no longer good for anything, except to be thrown out and trampled under foot by men" (Matt. 5:13).

## Our Immoral Circumstances

In our current environment we are facing a number of moral issues that are politically-charged. Some of these are issues directly affecting

---

[14] John F. Walvoord in Charles Lee Feinberg, ed. *Prophecy and the Seventies* (Chicago: Moody, 1971), 43.

[15] Walvoord in Feinberg, *Prophecy and the Seventies*, 212.

[16] Wayne House and Thomas D. Ice, *Dominion Theology: Blessing or Curse?* (Eugene, Ore.: Multnomah, 1988), 340.

[17] John F. MacArthur, *The Vanishing Conscience: Drawing the Line in a No-Fault, Guilt-Free World* (Dallas, Tex.: Word, 1994), 12.

[18] Rousas John Rushdoony, "Christian Missions And Indian Culture," *Westminster Theological Journal,* 12:1 (Nov., 1949): 2.

our everyday lives here in America; others involve issues appearing in other cultures and nations of our world which can indirectly affect our own political situation.

Like the demon Christ confronted (Mark 5:9), the moral issues the world faces today are Legion. They include: convenience abortions, neonatal infanticide, doctor-assisted suicide, homosexual relationships, non-marital childbearing, sexual promiscuity, sexual cohabitation, family breakdowns, latch-key children, child abuse, domestic violence, reproductive cloning, embryonic research, genetic engineering, organ farming, racial discrimination, human trafficking, rampant criminality, drug trafficking, substance abuse, rampant pornography, Islamic terrorism, cultural genocide, forced slavery, political torture . . . and more.

Obviously I cannot deal with all of these issues in this one short chapter. So I will have to focus on one, pressing moral problem by way of explaining and illustrating our precarious social and political circumstances, while highlighting the pattern of Christian political concern.

Thankfully many Christians have been battling abortion for several decades, so that this issue is well-known to the Christian community and well-represented in political battles. This is literally a political life-and-death issue. Christians must continue in this battle against abortions since it destroys innocent human lives for mere convenience. Furthermore, a tragic side-effect of abortion rates in America is that abortion is effectively causing black genocide. A February 24, 2010 CNN report backed up a prior ABC report noting this problem. Matthew Balan commented on CNN's observation regarding the high figures for black abortions:

> "Those figures that you cite from 2008 would seem to be in line with the CDC findings- Centers for Disease Control findings — from 2006, which found 57.4 percent of abortions in Georgia were performed on black women, even though African-Americans only make up 30 percent of the population."[19]

---

[19] Matthew Balan, "CNN Joins ABC in Highlighting Blacks' High Abortion Rate" (2/24/10). See the full article at: http://newsbusters.org/blogs/matthew-balan/ 2010/02/24/cnn-joins-abc-highlighting-blacks-high-abortion-rate

Since the abortion problem is well-known and long-battled, what I will do in this chapter is focus on one key moral issue of legal and political consequence: the homosexual rights revolution. This is a lively political debate that is intensifying almost daily. In fact, we are at a crucial time for confronting it, for it may be our last opportunity to resist it. I will mention the political significance for our time first, then focus on the dangers of the homosexual revolution.

We are at the very height of the homosexual revolution, and this means that we are at a crucial turning point for our culture and our nation. Most historians agree that the Gay Rights Movement was ignited on June 28, 1969. On that date forty years ago a series of spontaneous and violent demonstrations erupted against an early morning police raid of a gay bar. This episode became known as the Stonewall Riots in that the raided bar was the Stonewall Inn located in the Greenwich Village area of New York City.

We have come a long way since then. Today the list of homosexual victories continues to grow, from repealing sodomy laws and legal recognition of the right to marry the same sex, to adopt children, to serve openly in the military, to seek government funding for sex change operations, and more. This explosive change should not have been unexpected. In 2004 Robert Benne and Gerald McDermott warned:

"It is a superficial kind of individualism that does not recognize the power of emerging social trends that often start with only a few individuals bucking conventional patterns of behavior. Negative social trends start with only a few aberrations. Gradually, however, social sanctions weaken and individual aberrations became a torrent."[20]

Today we are under a full-scale, frontal assault from the left and homosexual-rights advocates. In an article titled "Is the Gay Marriage Debate Over?" Mark Galli noted:

"Seemingly out of nowhere, gay marriage advocates have won stunning judicial, legislative, and social victories. Connecticut began granting marriage certificates to spouses of the same gender in November 2008. In April 2009, Iowa's high court ruled that banning gay marriages was

---

[20] Robert Benne and Gerald McDermott, "Speaking Out: Why Gay Marriage Would Be Harmful," *Christianity Today* (February 1, 2004). http://www.christianity today.com/ct/2004/februaryweb-only/2-16-41.0.html

unconstitutional, and gay couples began lining up at Iowa court houses. The Vermont legislature legalized gay marriage that same month, while Maine and New Hampshire legalized gay marriage in May."[21]

On June 26, 2015, same-sex marriage was legalized in America by the U. S. Supreme Court's Obergefell v. Hodges decision. Historically, the Dutch parliament passed the first national legislation to allow same-sex marriage and adoption in December, 2000. In rapid succession after that, homosexual marriage became a legal right in Belgium (2003), Spain (2005), Canada (2005), South Africa (2006), Norway (2008), Sweden (2009), Argentina (2010), Portugal (2010), and Iceland (2010).

The Internet even boasts a number of "Christian" gay sites. One such site, ChristianGays.com boldly states:

"Christian Gays is a community for ALL, including LGGBTTIQQEU2AA (Lesbian, Gay, Genderqueer, Bisexual, Transgender, Transsexual, Intersex, Queer, Questioning, Eunuch, Undecided, 2-Spirited, Asexual, and Allied), and while we are absolutely Christian-based, we also believe strongly in Christ's acceptance and support of all, so you will find information and support here for faiths other than Christianity. We range in age from 13–96."[22]

As Christians concerned for our nation, we must recognize the moral collapse going on all around us. And where appropriate, we must confront these matters in the political realm. Homosexual rights is certainly one of the leading moral-political issues of our times.

### Our Current Concerns

In this section of our study I will present a few of our current concerns regarding the homosexual revolution. This will provide only a quick survey of the sort of problems we face. But if we are truly concerned about the moral and legal direction our nation and our government are heading, these should spark our commitment to political engagement. As

[21] Mark Galli, "Is The Gay Marriage Debate Over?," *Christianity Today* (July 24, 2009). http://www.christianitytoday.com/ct/2009 july/34.30.html
[22] "Who Are We And Why Do We Exist?" See home page at: http://christian-gays.com/

noted in the Preface much of this material has not been updated since 2012. But keeping these comments as they were, we will see that our worst fears are being realized.

### Biblical concerns

As Christians our core concern should be biblical because "Your word is truth" (John 17:17). As noted previously morality is rooted in religious truth, and for the Christian that truth is found in Scripture. So what does the Bible have to say about homosexual conduct?[23] Despite liberal attempts to re-interpret biblical condemnations of homosexual actions, God's word is clear.

The earliest recorded, direct statement on homosexuality in the New Testament appears in 1 Corinthians:

> "do you not know that the unrighteous will not inherit the kingdom of God? Do not be deceived; neither fornicators, nor idolaters, nor adulterers, nor effeminate, nor homosexuals, nor thieves, nor the covetous, nor drunkards, nor revilers, nor swindlers, will inherit the kingdom of God." (1 Cor. 6:9–10)

This statement deals with God's evaluation of (unrepentant) homosexuals and regards their salvation.

In Romans 1 Paul condemns homosexuality as it comes to expression in society. He declares that homosexual conduct is biologically unnatural, morally depraved, socially indecent, and culturally degrading :

> "For this reason God gave them over to degrading passions; for their women exchanged the natural function for that which is unnatural, and in the same way also the men abandoned the natural function of the woman and burned in their desire toward one another, men with men committing indecent acts and receiving in their own persons the due penalty of their error. And just as they did not see fit to acknowledge

---

[23] We must distinguish between homosexual conduct (objective, external actions) and homosexuality (subjective, internal desires). Law cannot legislate against immoral desires, but only immoral actions. Although God can look on the heart and judge matters within, man cannot: "God sees not as man sees, for man looks at the outward appearance, but the LORD looks at the heart" (1 Sam. 16:7b; cp. 1 Kgs. 8:39; 1 Chron. 28:9; Prov. 21:2; Luke 16:15; Acts 1:24; 15:8; Rom. 8:27).

God any longer, God gave them over to a depraved mind, to do those things which are not proper." (Rom. 1:26–28)

In one of Paul's last writings he declares that God's law condemns homosexual conduct and subjects it to judicial review so that it might be curtailed. And he even declares that such condemnation is an aspect of "sound teaching" and the "gospel":

> "But we know that the Law is good, if one uses it lawfully, realizing the fact that law is not made for a righteous person, but for those who are lawless and rebellious, for the ungodly and sinners, for the unholy and profane, for those who kill their fathers or mothers, for murderers and immoral men and homosexuals and kidnappers and liars and perjurers, and whatever else is contrary to sound teaching, according to the glorious gospel of the blessed God, with which I have been entrusted." (1 Tim. 1:8–11)

Paul's condemnation of homosexuality is rooted in his high view of God's law. He states that the law is given "so that *every mouth* may be closed and *all the world* may become accountable to God" (Rom. 3:19b). He does not see the law as contrary to the new covenant: "Do we then nullify the Law through faith? May it never be! On the contrary, we establish the Law" (Rom. 3:31). Indeed, he sees the law as an expression of the righteousness of God: "the Law is holy, and the commandment is holy and righteous and good" (Rom. 7:12). Spiritual sanctification moves Christians to live by standards of God's Law (Rom. 8:3–4), which defines who is truly a Christian (Rom. 8:7–8)

Thus we must look back to the Old Testament to see that God's law condemns homosexual conduct. In Leviticus 18:22 God expressly forbids such actions as morally reprehensible: "You shall *not* lie with a male as one lies with a female; it is an *abomination*." In fact, in Leviticus 20:13 he severely condemns homosexual activity: "If there is a man who lies with a male as those who lie with a woman, both of them have committed a *detestable* act; they shall surely be put to death. Their bloodguiltiness is upon them."

These are not Scripture's only prohibitions against homosexuality, but they are its leading, most direct ones (see: Gen. 19:1–25; Jdg. 19:22–30; 2 Pet. 2:6–10; Jude 7). They must impact the Christian worldview in that they are clear statements of God's evaluation of homosexual conduct.

Some writers attempt to circumvent the clear evidence summarized above by claiming that Jesus never condemned homosexual conduct. But this line of argument cannot stand close scrutiny.

First, such an argument is known as an "argument from silence." An argument from silence (technically called *argumentum ex silentio*) is a weak form of argument that is considered a logical fallacy when presented as a logical proof of something. If we apply this form of argument to Christ's teaching, he could be used to show that rape, cannibalism, bestiality, necrophilia, and other such conduct are acceptable since he never mentions them.

Second, we do not know whether Jesus ever mentioned homosexuality in any of his sermons and private discourses, for not everything he taught is recorded (John 21:25). For instance, Paul cites a statement by Jesus that is not found in the Gospel record: "remember the words of the Lord Jesus, that He Himself said, 'It is more blessed to give than to receive'" (Acts 20: 35b). Consequently, this claim regarding Christ cannot be substantiated.

Third, we do know that Jesus affirmed the law of God and even applied it *more deeply* than its surface statements suggested. In fact, he opens his ministry in his first major public discourse with an affirmation of God's law. In Matthew 5:17–19 we read:

> "Do not think that I came to abolish the Law or the Prophets; I did not come to abolish but to fulfill. For truly I say to you, until heaven and earth pass away, not the smallest letter or stroke shall pass from the Law until all is accomplished. Whoever then annuls one of the least of these commandments, and teaches others to do the same, shall be called least in the kingdom of heaven; but whoever keeps and teaches them, he shall be called great in the kingdom of heaven."

Here he expressly aligns his ministry with God's law and even rebukes anyone who would annul "one of the least of these commandments." He then goes on to deepen the implications of the law, for instance by noting that its prohibition of murder also prohibits hatred (Matt. 5:21–22) and its condemnation of adultery applies to lust (Matt. 5:27). In the same discourse he establishes the Golden Rule on the basis of "the Law and the Prophets" (Matt. 7:12; cp. Matt. 22:40; Rom. 13:8ff). How could we assume — on the basis of silence — that Jesus would tolerate homosexual conduct, which God's law expressly condemns?

Fourth, Jesus pointedly affirmed the ordinance of marriage as between a man and a woman. He even does this on the basis of the *Old Testament* revelation: "He answered and said, 'Have you not read that He who created them from the beginning made them male and female, and said, "for this reason a man shall leave his father and mother and be joined to his wife, and the two shall become one flesh'?" (Matt. 19:4–6).

Finally, Christ called, commissioned, and authorized his apostles to teach; in fact, he directed them to teach "them to observe all that I commanded you" (Matt. 28:19) and promised them his Spirit to guide them into all truth, some of which they have not yet received (John 16:12–13). He personally appeared to Paul to commission him as an apostle (Acts 9:1–6, 15; Gal. 1:1, 11–12). This is significant in that his commissioned apostles condemned homosexuality (Rom. 1:18–21; 1 Cor. 6:9–11; 1 Tim. 1:8–11; 2 Pet. 2:6–10).

Clearly, homosexuality and homosexual conduct are contrary to God's revelation. It is therefore contrary to the Christian worldview.

## Moral concerns

Since morality is rooted in a transcendent standard and is thereby inherently religious, and since God is that ultimate standard, I have been showing in this chapter that his word must govern our morality. I am further arguing that Christians must listen to its religious and moral standards then promote them in the legal and political sphere. This is terribly important in that, as prominent political theorist and social critic Russell Kirk noted: "to cut off Law from its ethical sources is to strike a terrible blow at the rule of law."[24]

For hundreds of years in Western Christian culture, homosexual desires have been deemed immoral and homosexual conduct judged as criminal. In fact, "before 1970, most psychiatrists adhered to the common wisdom of the day: homosexuality was immoral and an indication of some sort of defect in the individual."[25] But today our Christian-based cultural mores are being overthrown with a vengeance.

---

[24] Russell Kirk, "The Christian Postulates of English and American Law," *Journal of Christian Jurisprudence* (Tulsa, Okla.: O. W. Coburn School of Law, 1980), 66.

[25] Patricia H. Bazemore, "Homosexuality," Medscape Reference (August 4, 2011). http://emedicine.medscape.com/article/293530- overview#aw2aab6b5

Disestablishing the moral order of civilization undermines and endangers the culture it represents. When a culture is untethered from its moral traditions it begins to drift and becomes unstable, opening the door to a further collapse of moral values by the evaporation of standards of right and wrong. We see this in the rapid progress of the homosexual agenda. And in my third point below, I will show how God's word warns against this tragic reality noting that it is a form of divine judgment in a rebellious social order.

The unwinding of our traditional moral order not only alters our culture's moral compass, but is now destabilizing the very cornerstone of human society: marriage. For thousands of years Western culture has accepted marriage as subsisting only between a man and a woman. But now with the radical and militant promotion of homosexual marriage our understanding of the marriage institution itself is collapsing.

To make matters worse, research shows that homosexual unions are not as "confining" as traditional marriage relationships. Committed homosexual relationships allow for a greater openness toward outside liaisons. And according to a study in the Netherlands where homosexual revolution is virtually complete, the length of homosexual relationships generally last about eighteen months.[26] Marriages today have already been destabilized by other cultural pressures and political legislation (such as no-fault divorce). But once homosexual marriages as understood in homosexual communities becomes a part of our culture, we will be sliding into open marriages.

As the social foundation of our cultural and moral order is shaken by reinventing marriage, then the door is pushed open to further abuses. What is to stop polygamous marriages? polyandrous marriages (one wife with several husbands)? fraternal polyandry (several brothers having the same wife)? plural marriages? group marriage (several husbands possessing several wives with no primary core couple)? polyamory (legal and consensual acceptance of more than one intimate relationship simultaneously)? temporary marriages (serial monogamy)? child marriage? ghost marriage (allowing someone to marry a deceased person to continue a name or to secure wealth)? human-animal marriage? the repeal of

---

[26] Maria Xiridou, et al, "The Contribution of Steady and Casual Partnerships to the Incidence of HIV Infection among Homosexual Men in Amsterdam," *AIDS* 17 (2003): 1031.

laws against bigamy? the dissolving of marriage altogether in a culture of free love allowing indiscriminate promiscuity?

Where will it stop? Probably the most likely conclusion to this moral erosion of the family is in polyamory for it best fits an amoral culture. In fact, a scholarly movement is afoot that is enthusiastic regarding "a social revolution that would replace traditional marriage and family law."[27]

**Cultural concerns**

I have already indicated the cultural dangers in a society of collapsing morals. But here I want to bring in the biblical warning against such, then make just a brief comment on the observations of a few scholars.

In Romans 1 Paul warns Roman Christians that God stands as a judge over human societies. When a culture turns against God, he will only endure them for so long; he will eventually turn a God-denying culture over to its own base desires. The consequent surge in immorality becomes a sign of the end of that culture. Significantly, Paul highlights rampant homosexuality as evidence of God's judgment:

> "Therefore God gave them over in the lusts of their hearts to impurity, so that their bodies would be dishonored among them. For they exchanged the truth of God for a lie, and worshiped and served the creature rather than the Creator, who is blessed forever. Amen. For this reason God gave them over to degrading passions; for their women exchanged the natural function for that which is unnatural, and in the same way also the men abandoned the natural function of the woman and burned in their desire toward one another, men with men committing indecent acts and receiving in their own persons the due penalty of their error." (Rom. 1:24–27)

Homosexual conduct is the moral issue Paul uses to signal the decline and fall of a civilization. The next verses following this paragraph show that cascading immorality follows:

> "And just as they did not see fit to acknowledge God any longer, God gave them over to a depraved mind, to do those things which are not proper, being filled with all unrighteousness, wickedness, greed, evil; full of envy, murder, strife, deceit, malice; they are gossips, slanderers, hat-

---

[27] "The Marriage Amendment: Editorial" *First Things* 136 (October 1, 2003): 1048.

ers of God, insolent, arrogant, boastful, inventors of evil, disobedient to parents, without understanding, untrustworthy, unloving, unmerciful; and although they know the ordinance of God, that those who practice such things are worthy of death, they not only do the same, but also give hearty approval to those who practice them." (Rom. 1:28–32)

When a culture continually resists God, he abandons it to rampant homosexuality. This abandonment opens the floodgates of a deluge of other immoralities, a number of which Paul lists in these verses.

This forecast of a collapsing civilization is born out by modern studies. In 1947 the late Carle Zimmerman, Professor of Sociology at Harvard University, wrote his magnum opus titled *Family and Civilization*.[28] In that work he studied the decline of a number of civilizations, noting eight patterns of conduct that signaled their collapse. Several of these had to do with the family; the spread of homosexuality was another one. Arnold J. Toynbee concurred in his twelve-volume *A Study of History* (1934–61), noting famously that "civilizations die from suicide, not from murder."

In fact, according to evangelical theologian Al Mohler:

> "Pitirim Sorokin, the founder of sociology at Harvard University, pointed to the regulation of sexuality as the essential first mark of civilization. According to Sorokin, civilization is possible only when marriage is normative and sexual conduct is censured outside of the marital relationship. Furthermore, Sorokin traced the rise and fall of civilizations and concluded that the weakening of marriage was a first sign of civilizational collapse."[29]

### Spiritual concerns

Due to the psychologizing of so much law today, and given the modern tendency to political correctness, continuing to pass pro-homosexual legislation will negatively impact individual Christians, established churches, and religious ministries. The spiritual ministry of Christianity in our nation will be curtailed and threatened — then thwarted and condemned.

---

[28] Carle Zimmerman, *Family and Civilization,* ed. by James Kurth (2d. ed.: Wilmington, Del.: Intercollegiate Studies Institute, 2008).

[29] Albert Mohler, "Al Mohler, "The Case Against Homosexual Marriage," at Crosswalk.com (Jan. 15, 2004). http://www.crosswalk. com/news /al-mohler/ the-case-against-homosexual-marriage-1241113.html

A recent *Washington Times* news release reported on a national meeting of forty religious leaders. The article was titled: "Religious leaders: Gay marriage a peril to liberty."[30] This report noted that these religious leaders released an open letter warning that "the battle against same-sex marriage is a fight on behalf of religious freedom." One of the participants interviewed lamented that "marriage and religious liberty are at a crisis point in the United States."

The article also stated that "the 'most urgent peril' associated with legalizing same-sex unions is that religious individuals and organizations would be forced or pressured to treat same-sex sexual conduct as the moral equivalent of marital sexual conduct." This fear was earlier expressed in a *Christian Post* article which described the legal impact as "forcing Christian or other religious workers to be forced to adapt their business policies to accept a pro-gay agenda. There have already been several lawsuits against Christian business owners who refuse to serve homosexual couples due to religious beliefs."[31]

Harry Jackson and Tony Perkins point out that a U. S. House bill titled "Local Law Enforcement Hate Crimes Prevention Act of 2007" (H.R. 1592) would have granted special status to "sexual orientation" and "gender identity." They argue that once this is accomplished, pastors and churches could be prosecuted for preaching against homosexuality, since homosexuals would be a protected minority.[32] This would almost certainly prohibit churches from deposing pastors or excommunicating members for homosexual conduct, forbid them from "discriminating" against homosexuals in their hiring and ordaining practices, require that ministers perform homosexual marriages, and more.

Regarding the H. R. 1592 bill, Gudrun Schultz noted that:

---

[30] Cheryl Wetzstein, "Religious Leaders: Gay Marriage a Peril to Liberty," *Washington Times* (Jan. 12, 2012). http://www.washingtontimes. com/news/ 2012/ jan/12/religious-leaders-gay-marriage-a-peril-to-liberty/

[31] Amanda Winkler, "New Poll Says Majority of Americans Favor Same-Sex Marriage: Recent Votes on Marriage Amendments Tell a Different Story," *Christian Post* (Sept. 14, 2011). http://www.christianpost.com/news/new-polls-says- majority -of-americans-favor-same-sex-marriage-55624/

[32] Harry R. Jackson, Jr. and Tony Perkins, *Personal Faith, Pubic Policy* (Lake Mary, Fla.: Frontline, 2008), 165.

"Chuck Colson, founder of Prison Fellowship, in a BreakPoint Commentary warned that similar laws in England, Sweden and Canada have already resulted in the prosecution of Christians for hate crimes when they objected to homosexuality.

"'If this dangerous law passes, pastors who preach sermons giving the biblical view of homosexuality could be prosecuted,' Colson stated. 'Christian businessmen who refuse to print pro-gay literature could be prosecuted. Groups like Exodus International, which offer therapy to those with unwanted same-sex attraction, could be shut down.... Perhaps most frightening is the fact that liberal legislators have refused any amendment which would substantively protect religious expression in association with this legislation. Similar laws have been used around the world — and right here at home — to silence opposition to the homosexual lifestyle.'"[33]

The spiritual impact of such legislation would enormously hamper Christian ministry and threaten church ministers.

### Educational concerns

The American public education system today tends to focus less on academic issues and more on social engineering. Consequently, schools are too often used as an instrument for promoting the latest humanist value system. Concerned critics of our education system note that "what has clearly been on the rise in recent decades is the use of America's public schools for the purpose of engineering some social outcome deemed desirable by political leaders."[34] Political correctness rather than academic achievement is the driving engine of much education today.

At many teacher training classes and workshops "taxpayers are helping teachers learn new techniques for advancing the cause of 'social justice' in classrooms from kindergarten to college."[35] Children should be educated in the basic academic disciplines necessary for succeeding in

---

[33] Gudrun Schultz, "Dr. Dobson, Pro-life Groups Warn Sexual Orientation 'Hate Crime' Law Threatens Religious Freedom" (May, 2007) http://www. lifesitenews.com/news/archive/ldn/2007/may/07050207

[34] John Hood, "The Failure of American Public Education," *The Freeman* (Feb. 1993). http://www.thefreemanonline.org/columns/the-failure-of-american-public-education/

[35] Mary Grabar, "Training Teachers to Promote 'Social Justice,'" *Restore Oklahoma Public Education* (May 31, 2010). http://www.restoreokpubliceducation.com/node/573

the modern world, not indoctrinated according to humanist values and thrown into the front-lines of social reform and cultural transformation.

This becomes all the more remarkable in that we are witnessing a continual decline in academic test scores:

> "Anybody paying attention to the course of modern school reform will not be very surprised by this news: Newly released SAT scores show that scores in reading, writing and even math are down over last year and have been declining for years. And critical reading scores are the lowest in 40 years."[36]

> "The mean SAT reading scores of U.S. high schoolers have fallen to their lowest levels in nearly 40 years, dropping four points in the last four years to 497. Furthermore, only 43 percent of test takers achieved a total score indicating they are likely to succeed in college."[37]

This problem will not be helped by schools continuing to be distracted by political correctness and social engineering. And adopting the homosexual agenda is exacerbating the problem. A Mission America purpose statement puts the matter sharply:

> "The legalization of same sex liaisons as 'marriage' in the U.S would drastically alter the nature of what is taught to children in schools, community groups, camps, churches and in the media.
> "Currently, a high-pressure campaign by homosexual activists, supported by the National Education Association, is underway to promote acceptance of homosexuality among children, and a great deal of headway has already been made through the establishment of homosexual clubs, adoption of pro-homosexual school policies, the showcasing of homosexual literature, special occasion speakers, and so-called anti-bias programs. This revolutionary approach has received little mainstream publicity, but is rapidly gaining acceptance in educational circles

---

[36] Valerie Strauss, "What the Decline in SAT Scores Really Means," *Washington Post* (Sept. 13, 2011). http://www.washingtonpost.com/blogs/answer-sheet/post/what-the-decline-in-sat-scores-really-means/2011/09/14/gIQAdUzdSK_blog.html

[37] Steven Mintz, "Are Schools Being Held Accountable for Declining Test Scores?," *Ethics Sage* website (Sept. 23, 2011). http://www.ethicssage.com/2011/09/the-ethics-of-school-accountability-in-my-last-blog-i-pointed-out-that-the-mean-sat-reading-scores-of-us-high-schoolers-h.html

as the 'norm.' Recent laws enacted in California have basically mandated pro-homosexual teaching in state schools."[38]

To make matters worse, not only are academics declining, but sexual experimentation is increasing. And some of it is related to the educational focus on homosexual issues:

"There is growing evidence that bisexual identity and practices are developing as a popular trend among some middle school and high school students as a result of the promotion of homosexual experimentation. The 'package' of fluid sexual practices, featuring oral sex, is being sold to kids through many sex education programs and the popular culture. This trend has disastrous public health implications."[39]

Not only so, we are beginning to see stories reporting Christian students being disciplined when they mention their disagreement with homosexuality. Two recent news items highlight the problem of reverse discrimination.

"An honors student in Fort Worth, Texas, was sent to the principal's office and punished for telling a classmate that he believes homosexuality is wrong. . . . Dakota was sentenced to one day in-school suspension – and two days of full suspension."[40]
"A Catholic student who was bullied and vilified as a "bigot" for telling a teacher he was offended by homosexuality has filed a lawsuit against the Howell Public School District in Howell, Michigan."[41]

In November 2008 at Los Angeles Community College a student was giving a required speech for a Speech 101 class. That speech was supposed to be an informative speech on a topic of the student's interest.

---

[38] "Same Sex 'Marriage', Homosexuality, and the Education of Children: A Statement of Purpose By Mission America." http://www.mission america. com/purpose1.php

[39] "Same Sex 'Marriage', Homosexuality, and the Education."

[40] Todd Starnes, "Texas School Punishes Boy for Opposing Homosexuality," FoxNews.com. http://www.foxnews.com/us/2011/09/22/texas-school -punishes-boy-for-opposing-homosexuality/

[41] S. Brinkman, "Catholic Student Bullied for Views on Homosexuality Sues School," *Women of Grace* (Dec. 30, 2011). http://www.womenofgrace. com/ blog /?p=11198

Jonathan Lopez spoke of his Christian faith and how the Bible forbad homosexual marriages. According to Lopez, the professor stopped the speech, called him a "fascist bastard," refused to give him a grade, and attempted to have him expelled from school.[42]

The left-leaning educational establishment will continue to promote the homosexual agenda, unless our political direction is changed. This agenda is militantly promoting same-sex marriage, Lesbian-Gay-Bisexual-Transgender adoption, protecting sexual orientation as a civil rights minority classification, LGBT military participation, promoting LGBT history in public education. James Dobson well-expressed these concerns, noting the role of education:

> "Those goals include universal acceptance of the gay lifestyle, discrediting of scriptures that condemn homosexuality, muzzling of the clergy and Christian media, granting of special privileges and rights in the law, overturning laws prohibiting pedophilia, indoctrinating children and future generations through public education, and securing all the legal benefits of marriage for any two or more people who claim to have homosexual tendencies."[43]

The political direction our country is moving will not change without Christians actively participating in the political process.

**Political concerns**

Not long ago Supreme Court Justice Antonin Scalia dissented in the Lawrence v. Texas (2003) case, stating that: "Today's opinion is the product of a Court, which is the product of a law-profession culture, that has largely signed on to the so-called homosexual agenda, by which I mean the agenda promoted by some homosexual activists directed at eliminating the moral opprobrium that has traditionally attached to homosexual conduct."[44]

This problem of promoting the homosexual agenda had been made clear in a previous Supreme Court decision that set the stage for Law-

---

[42] Gale Holland, "Student Sues L.A. City College District over Gay-marriage Speech," *Los Angeles Times* (Feb. 16, 2009). http://articles.latimes.com/ 2009/feb/16/local/me-speech16

[43] James Dobson Family News (April, 2004). http://www.cft.org.za/articles/dobson.htm

[44] "Lawrence v. Texas," 539 U.S. 558 (2003).

rence v. Texas. In 1996 the landmark Romer v. Evans case struck down a recently passed amendment to the Colorado state constitution. That amendment would have prevented any Colorado city, town or county from taking any legislative, executive, or judicial action to declare homosexual citizens to be a protected class. The amendment basically established that homosexuals would be treated like any other citizens and not given special rights and protections. In his dissent, Scalia wrote that this amendment was "a modest attempt by seemingly tolerant Coloradans to preserve traditional sexual mores against the efforts of a politically powerful minority to revise those mores through use of the laws. That objective, and the means chosen to achieve it, are . . . unimpeachable under any constitutional doctrine hitherto pronounced."

Not only are homosexuals receiving preferential treatment today, but we are in fact an increasing number of attacks on Christians who do not bow to the homosexual agenda. For instance, in a *Washington Post* article in 2009 we read of the following problems arising for Christians:

- A Christian photographer was forced by the New Mexico Civil Rights Commission to pay $6,637 in attorney's costs after she refused to photograph a gay couple's commitment ceremony.

- A psychologist in Georgia was fired after she declined for religious reasons to counsel a lesbian about her relationship.

- Christian fertility doctors in California who refused to artificially inseminate a lesbian patient were barred by the state Supreme Court from invoking their religious beliefs in refusing treatment.

- A Christian student group was not recognized at a University of California law school because it denies membership to anyone practicing sex outside of traditional marriage.[45]

---

[45] Jacqueline L. Salmon, "Faith Groups Increasingly Losing Legal Battles Over Gay Rights," *The Washington Post* (April 10, 2009) http://www.washington post.com/wp-dyn/content/article/2009/04/09/AR2009040904063.html

In an editorial by Michael Brown we learn the following[46]:

- On September 27, 2011, the Culturewatch website cited a report from the UK that, "Jamie Murray was warned by two police officers to stop playing DVDs of the New Testament in his café following a complaint from a customer that it was inciting hatred against homosexuals. Mr Murray, 31, was left shocked after he was questioned for nearly an hour by the officers, who arrived unannounced at the premises. He said he had turned off the Bible DVD after an 'aggressive inquisition' during which he thought he was going to be arrested and 'frog-marched out of the café like a criminal.'"

- Dr. Kenneth Howell, an adjunct professor at the University of Illinois, was fired in 2010 "after a student complained that he was 'offended' by Howell's academic discussion of the Catholic Church's position on homosexual behavior in an Introduction to Catholicism course. The student was not even enrolled in the class."

- Vicki Knox, a special education teacher at Union High School in New Jersey with 20 years of experience, was suspended because of anti-homosexuality comments she posted on her personal Facebook page. She was upset because a display board was put up in her school celebrating Lesbian Gay Bi Transgender History Month, expressed her disapproval on her Facebook page, along with her abhorrence of homosexuality. (She also expressed her strong Christian faith.)

These sorts of problems will only accelerate as our government succumbs to the radical left's social pressures. We can look in our own backyard at what is happening in the political world around us. According to James Dobson:

---

[46] Michael Brown, "Gay Rights Still Trumping Freedom of Speech, Religion," *Townhall.com*. http://townhall.com/columnists/michaelbrown/2012/01/25/gay_rights_still_trumping_freedom_of_speech_religion/page/full/

"Canada is leading the way on this revolutionary path. I could cite dozens of examples indicating that religious freedom in that country is dying. Indeed, on April 28, 2004, the Parliament passed bill C 250, which effectively criminalized speech or writings that criticize homosexuality. Anything deemed to be 'homophobic' can be punished by six months in prison or by other severe penalties.

"Pastors and priests in Canada are wondering if they can preach from Leviticus or Romans 1 or other passages from the writings of the apostle Paul. Will a new Bible be mandated that is bereft of 'hate speech'? Consider this: A man who owned a printing press in Canada was fined $3,400 for refusing to print stationary for a homosexual activist organization.

"Censorship is already in full swing. One of our Focus on the Family radio programs on the subject of homosexuality was judged by the Canadian Radio and Television Commission to be 'homophobic.' The radio station that carried the broadcast was censured for airing it, and I have not been able to address the issue since."[47]

Political correctness and the psychologizing of law are also leading in ever more dangerous directions. Now some scholars are declaring that pedophilia is inborn, a sickness that should not be treated as a crime. Indeed:

"Today virtually any unwanted behavior, from shopaholism and kleptomania to sexaholism and pedophilia, may be defined as a disease whose diagnosis and treatment belong in the province of the medical system. Disease-making thus has become similar to lawmaking....

"Mental health professionals are not the only 'progressives' eager to legitimize adult-child sex by portraying opposition to it as old-fashioned antisexual prejudice. In a 1999 article, Harris Mirkin, a professor of political science at the University of Missouri-Kansas City, stated that 'children are the last bastion of the old sexual morality.' As summarized by *The New York Times*, he argued that 'the notion of the innocent child was a social construct, that all intergenerational sex should not be lumped into one ugly pile and that the panic over pedophilia fit a pattern of public response to female sexuality and homosexuality, both of which were once considered deviant.' Mirkin cited precedents such as Greek pederasty. 'Though Americans consider intergenerational sex to be evil,'

---

[47] James Dobson, "Marriage Under Fire: Why We Must Win This Battle," *MNMarriage.com*. http://www.mnmarriage.com/docs/Why%20We%20Must%20 20 Win%20This%20Battle.pdf

he wrote, 'it has been permissible or obligatory in many cultures and periods of history.' He told the *Times*: 'I don't think it's something where we should just clamp our heads in horror.'"[48]

We see this elsewhere as pedophilia is being re-labeled by a more acceptable, more medical-sounding, more clinically-sanitized phrase: "Male Intergenerational Intimacy." Citing the *Journal of Homosexuality* (20:1/2, 1990) we learn that:

"In a recent lead article of the *Journal of Homosexuality* (1), for example, Harris Mirkin says the 'sexually privileged' have disadvantaged the pedophile through sheer political force in the same way that blacks were disadvantaged by whites before the civil-rights movement. . . .

"Gunter Schmidt decries discrimination against and persecution of pedophiles, and describes 'successful pedophile relationships which help and encourage the child, even though the child often agrees to sex while really seeking comfort and affection. These are often emotionally deprived, deeply lonely, socially isolated children who seek, as it were, a refuge in an adult's love and for whom, because of their misery, see it as a stroke of luck to have found such an 'enormously nurturant relation-ship.'" [49]

In another report we learn of a pedophilia conference where Dr. Fred Berlin of Johns Hopkins University gave the keynote address. One reporter who attended the conference noted the following statements made by the speakers:

- Pedophiles are "unfairly stigmatized and demonized" by society.
- There was concern about "vice-laden diagnostic criteria" and "cultural baggage of wrongfulness."
- "We are not required to interfere with or inhibit our child's sexuality."

---

[48] Thomas Szasz, "Sins of the Fathers: Is Child Molestation a Sickness or a Crime?." https://www.questia.com/magazine/1G1-89389298/sins-of-the-fathers-is-child-molestation-a-sickness

[49] Joseph Nicolosi, Ph.D. and Dale O'Leary, "On the Pedophilia Issue: What the APA Should Have Known," Thomas Aquinas Psychological Clinic, 2009. http://www.josephnicolosi.com/on-the-pedophilia-issue-what/

- "Children are not inherently unable to consent" to sex with an adult.
- "In Western culture sex is taken too seriously."
- "Anglo-American standard on age of consent is new [and 'Puritanical']. In Europe it was always set at 10 or 12. Ages of consent beyond that are relatively new and very strange, especially for boys. They've always been able to have sex at any age."
- An adult's desire to have sex with children is "normative."
- Our society should "maximize individual liberty. ... We have a highly moralistic society that is not consistent with liberty." "Assuming children are unable to consent lends itself to criminalization and stigmatization."
- "These things are not black and white; there are various shades of gray."
- A consensus belief by both speakers and pedophiles in attendance was that, because it vilifies MAPs, pedophilia should be removed as a mental disorder from the American Psychiatric Association's (APA) Diagnostic and Statistical Manual of Mental Disorders (DSM), in the same manner homosexuality was removed in 1973.
- Dr. Fred Berlin acknowledged that it was political activism, similar to the incrementalist strategy witnessed at the conference, rather than a scientific calculus that successfully led to the declassification of homosexuality as a mental disorder: The reason "homosexuality was taken out of DSM is that people didn't want the government in the bedroom," he said.
- The DSM ignores that pedophiles "have feelings of love and romance for children" in the same way adults love one another.
- "The majority of pedophiles are gentle and rational."
- The DSM should "focus on the needs" of the pedophile, and should have "a minimal focus on social control," rather than obsessing about the "need to protect children."[50]

---

[50] Nathan Tabor, "Johns Hopkins Hospital Supports Pedophilia?." https://canadafreepress.com/article/johns-hopkins-hospital-supports-pedophilia

## Conclusion

The evidence above warns of a "throne of destruction . . . which devises mischief by decree" (Psa. 94:20). In Psalm 58:1b–2 we hear the complaint: "Do you judge uprightly, O sons of men? / No, in heart you work unrighteousness; / On earth you weigh out the violence of your hands." Isaiah denounces wicked rulers: "Woe to those who enact evil statutes / And to those who constantly record unjust decisions" (Isa. 10:1). Isaiah almost seems to have our own judicial situation in mind when he writes: "No one sues righteously and no one pleads honestly. / They trust in confusion and speak lies; / They conceive mischief and bring forth iniquity" (Isa. 59:4). A few verses later he laments: "Justice is turned back, / And righteousness stands far away; / For truth has stumbled in the street, / And uprightness cannot enter" (Isa. 59:14).

As the homosexual revolution continues gaining momentum and racking up legal victories, we are seeing ever greater pressures on the political and judicial systems to fully-accept its radical agenda. Perhaps our greatest concern for our future as a nation should lie in who controls our court system. Presidents exercise a great and long-lasting power in appointing judges and Supreme Court justices.

As stated above regarding other contexts, we can see the danger of a suppression of the Christian and conservative witness in our land while our cultural moral degradation continues. Christians must become politically active and promote issues from within the context of their biblical worldview. We certainly cannot leave politics to the secularists who control the media, academia, and entertainment.

Chapter 4

# FOUNDATIONAL LAW

"To the law and to the testimony! If they do not speak according to this word, it is because they have no light." (Isa. 8:20)

### Introduction

In chapter 1 we saw that Christianity creates a worldview that arises from God's revelation in Scripture. This worldview is truly a *world* view — it must even guide us in our political endeavors. In chapter 2 we noted that Christianity did, as a matter of fact, impact the very founding and early political history of our nation. Thus, we see that our Christian worldview is not merely theoretical: it has had practical implications on America's history. In chapter 3 we noted governmental power must be established on moral standards. We saw there that Christianity is the only worldview that can provide a basis for universal, invariant, concrete, binding moral principles.

In this chapter we will take an additional step in our presentation of politics from a Christian perspective. We will now see that a just and stable government created from within a Christian worldview must be covenantal. Indeed, we have a *federal* system of government, and the Latin word *foedus* (from which we derive "federal") means "covenant." We must understand that biblical covenantalism serves as the model for and foundation of our constitutional republic.

As politically-concerned Christians citizens we must recognize the enormous significance of our U. S. Constitution. It is an important means (under God's providence) whereby Americans have enjoyed large-scale, and long-term safety, stability, liberty, and prosperity. Understanding the vital role of our Constitution in politics is crucial for engaging the political process — especially in a political setting that tends either to overlook the Constitution or re-work its meaning.

As we begin our analysis of our foundational law in this land possessing a strong Christian heritage, let us start with the Bible's own:

### Covenantal Backdrop

We find the idea of covenant spread throughout Scripture. The word "covenant" itself occurs 321 times in the Bible, with thirty-seven of those appearance in the New Testament. In fact, in the Bible's foundational book, Genesis, it appears early (Gen. 6:18) and often (twenty-six times; Gen. 6:18; 9:9ff; 15:18; 17:2ff; 21:27ff; 26:28; 31:44). In Scripture, covenants are established between men (e.g., Gen. 26:28; Exo. 23:32; 2 Sam. 3:12) and between God and man (e.g., Gen. 6:18; Gen. 17:7; Luke 22:20).

But what is a covenant?

### The meaning of covenant

Simply put, in the Bible a covenant is a formal agreement binding together two or more parties by establishing and declaring the stipulations, promises, privileges, and responsibilities involved in that relationship. It includes an historical prologue, solemn oaths, and formal witnesses. A covenant is usually secured by a written document that carefully and clearly outlines the expectations of the parties in agreement. For instance, God provides two tablets containing his Law — one for Israel and one for himself (Exo. 25:16, 21; 40:20; Deut. 10:1–5).

Regarding the published nature of God's covenant, in Deuteronomy 31:24–26 we read:

> "It came about, when Moses finished writing the words of this law in a book until they were complete, that Moses commanded the Levites who carried the ark of the covenant of the LORD, saying, 'Take this book of the law and place it beside the ark of the covenant of the LORD your God, that it may remain there as a witness against you. They were placed in the ark as a witness to Israel.'" (Deut. 31:24–26)

Covenants between God and man can differ from those between man and man in the way in which they are established. In divine covenants we must always recognize that God is the Absolute One. He therefore sovereignly and unilaterally establishes the terms of his covenant. For instance, we see this in God's covenant with Abraham:

> "I will establish My covenant between Me and you and your descendants after you throughout their generations for an everlasting covenant, to be God to you and to your descendants after you. I will give to you and to your descendants after you, the land of your sojournings, all the land of Canaan, for an everlasting possession; and I will be their God. God said further to Abraham, 'Now as for you, you shall keep My covenant, you and your descendants after you throughout their generations.'" (Gen. 17:7–9)

But human covenants may be effected in one of two basic ways. First, they may be *vassal treaties* (or suzerainty arrangements) between unequals, as when one nation "sovereignly" imposes its will on another through superior military force. We have examples of these in the famous Hittite suzerainty covenants in antiquity.

Second, covenants may be *parity agreements* between equals. These are mutually agreed upon for the common good of both parties. We see many samples of these in the Old Testament, such as the one between Jacob and Laban: "So now come, let us make a covenant, you and I, and let it be a witness between you and me" (Gen. 31:44). Marriage is also a common, familiar, and important covenantal relationship (Mal. 2:14–16).

The covenant idea is very important in Scripture, as we may surmise from the significance of the Abrahamic, Mosaic, Davidic, and other redemptive covenants. Covenants also have a strong impact on theology as they structure biblical doctrine. But our interest here is in the historical influence of covenant on our Constitution.

### The significance of theology

Historically, we should suspect the influence of biblical covenants on the American constitutional system. Generally we may do this by recalling the strong Christian influence on our founding and settling as a nation (see ch. 2). More specifically, though, we may surmise this through the specific religious convictions of our forefathers. It has been noted that "about two-thirds of the colonial population had been trained in the school of Calvin" through their Reformed theological heritage.[1] And "John Calvin's theological system served as the core belief structure of many colonial societies including Pilgrims, Puritans, Presbyterians, and Huguenots."[2]

As a consequence of our earliest settlers' numbers, convictions, and zeal, many historians hold that the effective father of America and its constitutional government is the great Reformed theologian John Calvin (e.g., Leopold Von Ranke, Merle D'Aubigne, Emilio Castelar, Douglas

---

[1] Loraine Boettner, *The Reformed Doctrine of Predestination* (Phillipsburg, N.J.: P & R, 1932), 382.

[2] Michael Streich, "Calvinism and Colonial Social Beliefs," *American History @ Suite 101*. http://michael-streich.suite101.com/calvinism-and-colonial-social-beliefs-a157766

Kelly, and Gregory Johnson[3]). Famed American historian George Bancroft (1800–1891), who wrote the most comprehensive history of colonial America in 1834, not only calls Calvin America's father, but states: "he who will not honor the memory and respect the influence of Calvin knows but little of the origin of American liberty."[4]

Though covenantalism as a theological system was not fully systematized until a century after Calvin, its seeds were planted by the great Reformer and were nurtured to maturity by Calvin's theological heirs.[5] We see the crucial role of covenant to the Calvinist theological system most clearly expressed in the Westminster Confession of Faith (especially ch. 7).

Now even more directly than our general history and religious complexion, we should note the legal foundation stone of democracy in America: the Mayflower Compact.[6] This Compact was itself a covenant document which expressly stated of its signers that we "covenant and combine ourselves together." In it these hardy Christians demonstrated a religious zeal for establishing a representative, democratic government recognizing that all parities had an equal investment. It reads:

> "IN THE NAME OF GOD, AMEN. We, whose names are underwritten, the Loyal Subjects of our dread Sovereign Lord King James, by the Grace of God, of Great Britain, France, and Ireland, King, Defender of the Faith, &c. Having undertaken for the Glory of God, and Advancement of the Christian Faith, and the Honour of our King and Country, a Voyage to plant the first Colony in the northern Parts of Virginia; Do by these Presents, solemnly and mutually, in the Presence of God and one another, covenant and combine ourselves together into a civil Body Politick, for our better Ordering and Preservation, and Furtherance of the

---

[3] John Eidsmoe, *Christianity and the Constitution: The Faith of Our Founding Fathers* (Grand Rapids: Baker, 1987), 18. Gregory Johnson, "The Many Faces of John Calvin: The Historiography of Calvin's Political Thought over Five Centuries," St. Louis University, Fall 1998. http://gregscouch.homestead.com/files/manyfaces. html#_ftn26

[4] George Bancroft, *The History of the United States* (Boston: Little, Brown, 1856), 390.

[5] See for example: "Richard L. Greaves, "The Origins and Early Development of English Covenant Thought," *The Historian* 31:1 (Nov. 1968): 21.

[6] *Congressional Record* (Washington: Government Printing Office, 1921), vol. 6, part 5, p. 4600.

Ends aforesaid: And by Virtue hereof do enact, constitute, and frame, such just and equal Laws, Ordinances, Acts, Constitutions, and Officers, from time to time, as shall be thought most meet and convenient for the general Good of the Colony; unto which we promise all due Submission and Obedience. IN WITNESS whereof we have hereunto subscribed our names at Cape-Cod the eleventh of November, in the Reign of our Sovereign Lord King James, of England, France, and Ireland, the eighteenth, and of Scotland the fifty-fourth, Anno Domini; 1620."

This covenantal concern was no passing fancy on their part, for as constitutional law professor John Eidsmoe notes: "in 1636 the General Court of Massachusets resolved to make a code of laws 'agreeable to the word of God.'"[7] Then in 1641 the first civil law code in American was adopted: the Massachusetts Body of Liberties, which even cited specific Bible verses to serve as the underpinnings of the laws.

The Hanover Historical Texts Projects provides us with the "History of the Manuscript":

"Another General Court assembled; and 'the Governor [Vane], Deputy -Governor [Winthrop], Thomas Dudley, John Haynes, Richard Bellingham, Esq., Mr. Cotton, Mr. Peter, and Mr. Shepard were entreated [May 25, 1636] to make a draft of laws agreeable to the word of God, which might be the fundamentals of this Commonwealth, and to present the same to the next General Court.' (Mass. Rec., I. 174.) Provisionally 'the Magistrates and their associates' were to 'proceed in the Courts to hear and determine all causes according to the laws now established; and where there is no law, then as near the law of God as they can. . . . At the time appointed [John Cotton] was all prepared, and 'did present a copy of Moses his judicials, compiled in an exact method, which were taken into further consideration till the next General Court.'"[8]

Those compiling and adopting this law code saw God's covenant law as a foundation to social order — and political "Libertie." This document opens:

"The free fruition of such liberties Immunities and priveledges as humanitie, Civilitie, and Christianitie call for as due to every man in his place

---

[7] Eidsmoe, *Christianity and the Constitution*, 32.

[8] "The Massachusetts Body of Liberties (1641)" by the Hanover Historical Texts Project (1996), http://history.hanover.edu/texts/masslib.html

and proportion without impeachment and Infringement hath ever bene
and ever will be the tranquillitie and Stabilitie of Churches and Common-
wealths. And the deniall or deprivall thereof, the disturbance if not the
ruine of both."

And this is how God intended his law to be used, for in Deuteronomy
4:5–6 we read Moses' words to Israel, where he presents her the law as
a model for the nations:

"See, I have taught you statutes and judgments just as the LORD my God
commanded me, that you should do thus in the land where you are
entering to possess it. So keep and do them, for that is your wisdom and
your understanding in the sight of the peoples who will hear all these
statutes and say, 'Surely this great nation is a wise and understanding
people.'"

Vincent Ostrom, the highly-regarded retired Professor of Political
Science at Indiana University, argues that "the American constitutional
tradition . . . implies a strong covenantal tradition. . . . The covenantal
tradition refers to circumstances like the Sinaitic tradition of the Hebrews."[9] Political science professor Daniel Elazar of Temple University has
written much on the biblical covenant and goes a step further. He points
out that it was a expressly used as a model for the U. S. Constitution.
Portions of his work should prove helpful to us at this point in our
study[10]:

"At the very beginning of the history of covenant there was the great
idea of biblical covenantal monotheism whereby humans were envisaged
as entering into morally grounded pacts with God out of which came,
*inter alia* ["among other things"], the covenant with Noah binding all of
humanity and that with the people Israel formed through the Exodus
from Egypt and the Sinai experience. In the sixteenth century Protestant
Reformation, a new theology of covenant gave rise to Reformed Protes-

---

[9] Vincent Ostrom, "Hobbes, Covenant, and Constitution," *Publius* 10:4 (Autumn, 1980), 83.
[10] Daniel J. Elazar, *The Covenant Tradition in Politics*, vol. 3 of *Covenant and
Constitutionalism: The Great Frontier and the Matrix of Federal Democracy* (Piscataway,
N. J.: Transaction, 1997). See: *Jerusalem Center for Public Affairs* website. http:
//www.jcpa.org/dje/books/ct-vol3-int.htm

tantism and the theo-political transformation that followed in countries such as Switzerland, the Netherlands, Scotland, and England. . . .

"What the combination of covenant theology, religious reformation, and local or national political transformation did for the sixteenth century, a revolution in political philosophy, . . . led to the Glorious Revolution of 1688-89, and the formation of the American colonies across the Atlantic on a Reformed Protestant base during that same period, did the same for the seventeenth century. . . ."

"Constitutionalism [was] a modern reinterpretation of the covenantal tradition that gave it flesh and blood and enabled it to become the instrument of liberty, equality, justice, and democracy that it did. Thus, for all of its flawed beginnings and flawed history, where Europeans were able to implant the covenantal tradition, the New World did indeed offer an opportunity, if not an entirely unambiguous one, for beginning again."

"Certain parts of the New World were settled by those who brought the covenant tradition with them. . . ."

"The generation that achieved the Declaration of Independence, fought the Revolutionary War, and established the United States under its new constitution was led by two groups: one coming out of the older religious tradition, primarily the covenantal tradition of Reformed Protestantism who saw the imperatives of their tradition leading in the direction of a federal democratic republic under God, and the second group who came out of the Enlightenment, influenced primarily by the Scottish Enlightenment which was part of the covenantal tradition one step removed, who sought a federal democratic republic in North America as the way to actualize civil society."

At this juncture we should note an important statement made be William Blackstone (1723–1780), famed British jurist who wrote his best-selling and enormously influential *Commentaries on the Laws of England* (published between 1765 and 1769). In these *Commentaries* Blackstone argued that "upon these two foundations, the law of nature and the law of revelation ["the Holy Scriptures"], depend all human laws; that is to say, no human law should be suffered to contradict these."[11]

Blackstone's statement is significant for our Constitutional history, for as Robert Ferguson (Professor of Law, Columbia University) comments:

---

[11] William Blackstone, *Commentaries on the Laws of England*, ed., by William Carey Jones (Baton Rouge: Claitor's, 1976), 42–43.

"All our formative documents — the Declaration of Independence, the Constitution, the Federalist Papers and the seminal decisions of the Supreme Court under John Marshall — were drafted by attorneys steeped in Sir William Blackstone's *Commentaries on the Laws of England.* So much was this the case that the *Commentaries* rank second only to the Bible as a literary and intellectual influence on the history of American institutions."[12]

Our political concerns as contemporary Christian citizens should reflect a high regard for our Constitution which arose out of an historically-Christian milieu. Our Constitution establishes a clear standard for procedural law, not a vague suggestion. But the Constitution is only as sure as its foundation. Historian Russell Kirk rightly warned us that "to cut off Law from its ethical sources is to strike a terrible blow at the rule of law."[13] And in America, constitutional law was established on a Christian and biblical foundation which is rooted in absolute, unchanging, and just principles for law.[14]

Thus, as John Sterling, Professor of Criminal Justice in the University of North Carolina system, observes:

"The United States of America was not born in a vacuum nor did it emerge from a single spasm of political or social reaction. The nation was, as Lincoln proclaimed at Gettysburg, 'conceived in liberty' long before the war with England for independence. What philosophical or historical writings influenced America's founding?... When one searches for underlying principles of self-government, it is not difficult to trace the historical origins back several thousand year — to the ancient Hebrews in the Old Testament of the Bible." [15]

---

[12] Robert A. Ferguson, *Law and Letters in American Culture* (Cambridge: Harvard University Press, 1984), 11.

[13] Russell Kirk, "The Christian Postulates of English and American Law," *Journal of Christian Jurisprudence* (Tulsa, Okla.: O. W. Coburn School of Law, 1980), 66.

[14] This is not to say that our Constitution is perfect or that it is absolute and unchanging. It is only to say that for it to function, we must recognize and maintain its covenantal roots.

[15] John A. Sterling, "A Look at the Philosophical Roots of American Constitutional Republicanism," *Law & Liberty* website. http://www.lawandliberty. org/history1.htm

## Constitutional Parallel

In that the historical roots of our Constitution ultimately derive from biblical covenants by way of our Christian forefathers, we should expect to find parallels between it and Scriptural covenants. Indeed, late Professor of Political Philosophy at Drew University, Neal Riemer has written an important article regarding this correlation: "Covenant and the Federal Constitution."[16]

Though not arguing for a direct historical linkage between the two, Riemer states early in his article that he notes "some striking similarities between the Sinai Covenant and the U.S. Constitution" (p. 135). He demonstrates that "the relationship between God and man becomes the model for all human relationships — individual, social, economic, political. By the terms of the covenant, human beings are obligated to act within certain limits" (p. 136).

As a consequence, "in each case — covenant and Constitution — a community, a people, a nation is established. The community becomes a lasting relationship" (Riemer, p. 139). In addition, "acceptance of the covenant obliges the people of Israel to fulfill the commandments. This is central to the covenantal relationship. . . . Similarly, the people of the several states — through the federal government they have established — are also committed to the fulfillment of the objectives of the Preamble" (pp. 139, 140).

Riemer's presentation "underscore[s] the fundamental contrast between a higher and lower law, with the lower subordinated to the higher. In the Sinai Covenant the contrast is between the divine and the human; divine law must prevail over human law if there is a conflict between the two. With regard to the U.S. Constitution, the contrast is between a superior and an inferior law. Federal law or action in conflict with the Constitution must fall. The Constitution is the higher standard used by Congress, president, courts, the several states" (p. 139).

In the final analysis, Reimer holds that covenant is an enduring legal relationship established between two or more parties. In the Bible the major covenants are between God and Israel. They promise a good life if Israel operates in terms of the covenant stipulations. The covenant harnesses powers in a written, public statement. Our Constitution performs

---

[16] Neal Riemer, "Covenant and the Federal Constitution," *Publius* 10:1 (Autumn, 1980): 135–48.

the same functions in the secular realm. The parallels between covenant and Constitution are strong.

This is significant for our political stability for as political scientist Daniel Elazar comments:

> "The Bible emphasizes communal liberty and what the Puritans in the seventeenth century defined as federal liberty, that is to say, the liberty to live up to the terms of the covenant (federal, from the Latin *foedus* meaning covenant), rather than individual liberty, which, as natural liberty, meant the lack of restraint except insofar as nature itself restrains us all."[17]

But now as politically-concerned Christian citizens, we must recognize our current political climate and the Constitution's:

### Judicial Danger

Though we have a clearly-written, long-standing Constitution (the oldest federal constitution in existence) we are witnessing its dissolution. Even liberal Supreme Court judges reject our Constitution. Consider the following recent news item:

> "Supreme Court Justice Ruth Bader Ginsburg has caused a storm of controversy by saying in a television interview that the people of Egypt should not look to the United States Constitution when drafting their own governing document because it's too old and there are newer examples from which to draw inspiration.
>
> 'I would not look to the U.S. Constitution if I were drafting a constitution in the year 2012,' Ginsburg said in the interview, which aired on Jan. 30 on Al-Hayat TV."[18]

How can we expect the Supreme Court to uphold Constitutional law if justices on that court deem the Constitution passe?

---

[17] Daniel J. Elazar, "Communal Democracy and Liberal Democracy in the Jewish Political Tradition," *Jerusalem Center for Public Affairs* website. http://www.jcpa.org/dje/articles/commdem-jpt.htm

[18] Alex Pappas, "Justice Ginsburg causes storm dissing the Constitution while abroad," *The Daily Caller* (Feb. 7, 2012). http://dailycaller.com/2012/02/06/justice-ginsburg-causes-storm-dissing-the-constitution-while -abroad/

As politically-concerned citizens we must be aware of this problem and employ our influence against the problem. But before I set up the matter, we need to recognize a doctrine that strongly influenced the writing of the Constitution.

## Our sinful tendencies

As we have noted, the Constitution arose out of a Christian milieu, one largely influenced by Calvinistic theology. One of the key Calvinistic doctrines undergirded our colonial forefathers' political concerns: the doctrine of man's inherent depravity. They firmly believed that man tends toward evil and that government leaders entrusted with political power must therefore be constrained. I will cite Madison and Jefferson in demonstrating this fact.

James Madison, who exercised a large influence on our Constitution, famously argued for "the partition of power" in government:

> "Ambition must be made to counteract ambition. The interest of the man must be connected with the constitutional rights of the place. It may be a reflection on human nature, that such devices should be necessary to control the abuses of government. But what is government itself, but the greatest of all reflections on human nature? If men were angels, no government would be necessary. If angels were to govern men, neither external nor internal controls on government would be necessary. In framing a government which is to be administered by men over men, the great difficulty lies in this: you must first enable the government to control the governed; and in the next place oblige it to control itself."[19]

In *The Federalist* #55 he wrote that "there is a degree of depravity in mankind which requires a certain degree of circumspection and distrust."

Even deist Thomas Jefferson held this understanding of man as crucial for framing a Constitution that would secure a free government with limited powers. In his "Kentucky Resolutions of 1798" he wrote:

> "Free government is founded in jealousy, and not in confidence; it is jealousy and not confidence which prescribes limited constitutions, to

---

[19] James Madison, "The Structure of the Government Must Furnish the Proper Checks and Balances Between the Different Departments," *Independent Journal* (Feb. 6, 1788). See text at: http://www.constitution.org/fed/federa51.htm

bind down those whom we are obliged to trust with power: that our Constitution has accordingly fixed the limits to which, and no further, our confidence may go; and let the honest advocate of confidence read the Alien and Sedition acts, and say if the Constitution has not been wise in fixing limits to the government it created, and whether we should be wise in destroying those limits, Let him say what the government is, if it be not a tyranny, which the men of our choice have conferred on our President, and the President of our choice has assented to, and accepted over the friendly stranger to whom the mild spirit of our country and its law have pledged hospitality and protection: that the men of our choice have more respected the bare suspicion of the President, than the solid right of innocence, the claims of justification, the sacred force of truth, and the forms and substance of law and justice. In questions of powers, then, let no more be heard of confidence in man, but bind him down from mischief by the chains of the Constitution."

This deeply-held suspicion of sinful man moved our forefathers to establish a government that included both a separation of powers (involving checks and balances between its branches) and a doctrine of express (therefore, limited) powers, and to secure these by a carefully written covenant (our Constitution). Though the British kings from whom they separated were often called "sovereigns," the Constitution never once uses the word "sovereign" in referring to governmental powers or offices. I will deal with this at length in chapter 5, but I must briefly mention governmental limitations at this point.

In Article 1, Section 8 of the Constitution we read of the "Powers vested by this Constitution."[20] This is the doctrine of express or enu

---

[20] Some hold that the statement "to make all Laws which shall be necessary and proper" is an elastic phrase that allows government more than the limited powers enumerated. However, the whole sentence ties this to the powers already granted, the expressly stated powers: "To make all Laws which shall be necessary and proper *for* carrying into Execution the *foregoing Powers,* and all other Powers *vested by this Constitution* in the Government of the United States, or in any Department or Officer thereof." Thomas Jefferson wisely commented that "it is an established rule of construction where a phrase will bear either of two meanings, to give it that which will allow some meaning to the other parts of the instrument, and not that which would render all the others useless." Thomas Jefferson, "Opinion on National Bank, 1791" in Andrew A. Lipscomb and Albery Ellery Bergh, *The Writings of Thomas Jefferson* (Washington, D.C.: Thomas Jefferson Memorial Association of the United States, 1903-04), 3:148. This quote and many

merated powers (powers expressly granted) at work. And the Constitution specifically limits federal power by adding in the Bill of Rights, Articles 9 and 10:

> "Amendment IX. The enumeration in the Constitution, of certain rights, shall not be construed to deny or disparage others retained by the people."
> "Amendment X. The powers not delegated to the United States by the Constitution, nor prohibited by it to the States, are reserved to the States respectively, or to the people."

As Neal Riemer notes in his work on the covenantal model for constitutionalism: "Constitutions do three things: (1) they limit power; (2) they grant power; and (3) they insist on due process in the exercise of legitimate — granted power."[21] Thus, he argues, "rightful power . . . is to be exercised, but within the framework of the Constitution's limitations, rule, requirements of due process. . . . The covenant explicitly places limits on what people can and cannot do. The Constitution does likewise" (p. 140).

Because of the sinfulness of the nation's leaders, unless constrained by the "chains" of a constitution they would impose chains on their citizens. For a constitution to have significance, laws should not contradict its express statements. Consistency and predictability must characterize a legal system. This is the whole point of a published constitution.

### Our Constitutional crisis

As just noted, constitutions are designed to grant, outline, and limit the use of powers in government. But in order to function properly, the specifics of a constitution must be known, understood, and followed. In contemporary law and politics this is no longer being done on an appreciable level.

Today we have court jurists and legal academics pushing an evolutionary meaning of the Constitution, deeming it a "living" document. As a living document it becomes a changing one that grows new, unexpec-

---

others on Jefferson's commitment to express powers can be found at: http://www.famguardian.org/Subjects/Politics/ThomasJefferson/jeff1020.htm

[21] Neil Reimer, "Covenant and the Federal Constitution," *Publius* 10:1 (Autumn, 1980): 137.

ted powers. This view operates on a loose construction of the Constitution based on a "dynamic" approach to its wording. This interpretive method is set over against the older "originalist" approach. Originalism demands that the original intent of the constitutional authors and the original meaning of their words must determine the proper understanding and guide the application of the Constitution today

Against the originalist school of thought on Constitutional interpretation, the living document approach may be divided into two camps: (1) The pragmatist camp deems the Constitution an old, outdated document no longer of practical use in the modern world. David A. Strauss in his recent book *The Living Constitution* (2010) puts the matter rather bluntly "the text of the Constitution will play, at most, a ceremonial role." He asks: "What possible justification can there be for allowing the dead hand of the past . . . to govern us today?" According to Strauss the Constitution "should be interpreted in the way best calculated to provide a point on which people can agree."[22]

(2) The intentionalist camp argues that the framers intentionally used broad language capable of flexible application. This approach urges that we read the Constitution contemporaneously (according to current moral, social, and culture climate) rather than historically (according to the original intent by its framers). This function of the Constitution was effectively established by Warren Court in its Trop v. Dulles decision in 1958. There the Supreme Court declared that the Constitution must comport with "evolving standards . . . that mark the progress of a maturing society."[23]

Ironically a "living" Constitution is actually a "dying" one, for it ceases to be what it was and is therefore effectively dead. A living Constitution is less like a living person (growing stronger under set genetic limitations) and more like a dead body (becoming compost in which all sorts of new and different plants take root and grow). This evolutionary approach to the interpretation of the Constitution reduces its principled and fixed meaning to a pragmatic and fluid one. As a consequence, we no longer have a law-based system but a lawyer-based system.

---

[22] See: Stanley Fish, "Why Bother With the Constitution?" *The New York Times* (May 10, 2010). http://opinionator.blogs.nytimes.com/2010/0510/why-bother-with -the-constitution/

[23] Trop V. Dulles, Secretary of State, 356 U.S. 86 (1958).

Michael Maharrey of the Tenth Amendment Center well notes that "Constitutional interpretation is not as mysterious and complicated as many would like to make it. The founders, framers and ratifiers wrote volumes on the subject, revealing not only the meaning of each article, but the principles underlying the document itself."[24]

Thomas Jefferson long ago summed up the situation nicely:

> "On every question of construction let us carry ourselves back to the time when the Constitution was adopted, recollect the spirit manifested in the debates, and instead of trying what meaning may be squeezed out of the text, or intended against it, conform to the probable one in which it was passed."[25]

He perceptively warned that "our peculiar security is in the possession of a written Constitution. Let us not make it a blank paper by construction."[26]

The problems arising from the concept of a living Constitution are many, varied, and dangerous. I will summarily list a few of them. Under this approach our Constitutionally-based legal system becomes:

- Unpredictable. Law ceases to be certain since there is no set meaning of the words in the Constitution.
- Unstable. It creates a fragile legal system allowing words and concepts to change their meaning as judges change their minds.
- Random. By the very nature of the case, loose construction can have no guiding principle to direct its evolutionary change — for any alleged guiding principle is itself subject to change.
- Contradictory. To accept the evolving meaning of Constitutional statements contradicts the very idea and purpose of a constitution as a set, written, and binding document which is a coherent and well-integrated body of laws

---

[24] Michael Maharrey, "How Should We Interpret the Constitution?" *Tenth Amendment Center* website. http://www.statebrief.com/briefblog/2010/09/24/how-should-we-interpret-the-constitution/

[25] Thomas Jefferson to William Johnson, 1823. Lipscomb and Bergh, *The Writings of Thomas Jefferson*, 15:449.

[26] Thomas Jefferson to Wilson Nicholas, 10:419.

- Tilted. Power shifts to the unelected judicial arm of govern-ment as it imposes new meanings on the Constitution under changing standards — as it pleases.

- Politicized. The law becomes politicized as it endures the subjective evaluations of any given judge appointed by a given political party. Through judges the law effectively "takes sides" in the culture war.

- Absurd. The Constitution has mechanisms in it for amending it, but the living Constitution approach allows amendment without using *those* clearly stated procedures, as if the court system was an on-going Constitutional Convention.

- Self-destructive. The loose construction approach encroaches on the Ninth and Tenth Amendments.[27] Giving the federal government new powers requires pulling them away from the Constitutionally-reserved rights and powers.

- Dangerous. With no set meaning of the words, our Constitu-tional rights become precarious. All Constitutionally-stated rights are on the table and subject to change by re-definition, including our rights to freedom of religion, free speech, assembly, etc.

- Difficult. Our Constitution is a rather compact (about 4400 words) and plainly written document easily accessible to the average citizen. A loose interpretation transforms it into a mysterious, deeply complex, open-ended legal code.

- Discouraging. Citizens become cynical of a law system that engages in self-contradiction and constant change.

Legal scholar and former Appeals Court Judge Robert Bork well states that:

"If the Constitution is law, then presumably its meaning, like that of all other law, is the meaning the lawmakers were understood to have

---

[27] The Ninth Amendment reads: "The enumeration in the Constitution, of certain rights, shall not be construed to deny or disparage others retained by the people." The Tenth Amendment reads: "The powers not delegated to the United States by the Constitution, nor prohibited by it to the States, are reserved to the States respectively, or to the people."

intended. If the Constitution is law, then presumably, like all other law, the meaning the lawmakers intended is as binding upon judges as it is upon legislatures and executives. There is no other sense in which the Constitution can be what article VI proclaims it to be: 'Law. . . .' This means, of course, that a judge, no matter on what court he sits, may never create new constitutional rights or destroy old ones. Any time he does so, he violates not only the limits to his own authority but, and for that reason, also violates the rights of the legislature and the people . . . the philosophy of original understanding is thus a necessary inference from the structure of government apparent on the face of the Constitution."[28]

The living Constitution argument is not only dangerous, it is unnecessary. Our Constitution is *not* a dead document, for it provides for a clearly stated process for ongoing amendment. Article 5 of the Constitution reads in part: "The Congress, whenever two thirds of both Houses shall deem it necessary, shall propose Amendments to this Constitution, or, on the Application of the Legislatures of two thirds of the several States, shall call a Convention for proposing Amendments."

Consequently, if changes are needed for modern culture and society, the Constitution secures for us a process by which we can effect those legitimately. As U. S. Supreme Court Justice Antonin Scalia points out: "The way to change the Constitution is through amendments approved by the people, not by judges altering the meaning of its words."[29] In fact, we have amended the Constitution twenty-seven times, with the first ten being our Bill of Rights and the last one being in 1992.

In point of fact, the loose construction argument is wrong on its very surface. The Preamble to our Constitution clearly shows that the framers intended to establish governmental law for the long run, for in it we read that the Constitution was ordained and established for "ourselves and our Posterity." They did not create nor did the nation adopt a constitutional document embodying designed obsolescence; they intended quite the opposite. If "Posterity" still means "posterity."

---

[28] Robert Bork, *The Tempting of America: The Political Seduction of the Law* (New York: Touchstone, 1991), 145.

[29] Peter J. Smith, "Justice Scalia Slams High Court for Inventing 'Living Constitution,' Right to Abortion," *LifeSiteNews* website (Nov. 23, 2010). http://www.lifesitenews.com/news/justice-scalia-slams-high-court-for-inventing-living-constitution-right-to/

## Conclusion

Our U.S. Constitution is not a God-breathed, infallible document. But it is the legal foundation of our nation that has not only helped make America the great power it is today, but has also granted us as Christians the right to our freedom of religion.

We need to treat it with respect and seek its implementation in modern legal and political discourse. Tragically today the Constitution is effectively dismissed as irrelevant by means of re-interpretation. The re-interpretation process has given us abortion as the national law of the land, opened the door to homosexual marriages which may eventually be imposed on all states by the Supreme Court, and more.

As worldview-oriented Christians concerned about our nation's political future, we must engage the political process and stand against Constitutional re-interpretation.

## Chapter 5
# LIMITED GOVERNMENT

"Render to Caesar the things that are Caesar's; and to God the things that are God's." (Matt. 22:21)

### Introduction

We saw in our last chapter that God deals with his people by way of covenant, and that the covenant concept provides a key foundation for a stable and just law order. We saw that historically covenantal theology even influenced our own Constitution.

In this chapter I will focus on one particularly important element of Christian-principled government: limited power. In our day of expansive governmental power we must be aware of the biblical constraints God intended for government. Because of the very real dangers of totalitarian government, we as Christians must engage the political process to exercise our influence for limited government. And to do this we must understand the biblical directives regarding these matters, as well as our Christian-influenced, Constitutional principles.

Let us begin first by considering the:

### Biblical Principles

As I have been noting throughout, God's word has much to say regarding politics. Apart even from the overtly political statements in Scripture, we may deduce this from our obligation as Christians. God has given us his word in order that we might be "*thoroughly* furnished for *every* good work" (2 Tim. 3:17b). We are commanded in that word: "*whatever* you do, do all to the glory of God" (1 Cor. 10:31). In fact, our Savior claimed for himself "*all* authority in heaven and on earth" (Matt. 28:18a). As a consequence of his possessing all authority, we are called to take "*every* thought captive to the obedience of Christ" (2 Cor. 10:5b). These statements demand that we live in terms of a *world*view, rather than a narrow "*church*view." Thus, in compelling us to seek God's glory in *all* of life, we must even engage the political realm as one particular — and important — area of life.

As we highlight the principle of limited government we must recognize:

### The source of authority

In our Bible-based worldview God is the one who alone possesses ultimate authority. This fact is established in principle in the opening words of Scripture. He is the Creator of all things, for Scripture teaches: "in the beginning God created the heavens and the earth" (Gen. 1:1; cp. Exo. 20:11; Acts 14:15; Rev. 4:11b).

Because God has created all things, he rightfully owns all things: "The earth is the LORD's, and all it contains, / The world, and those who dwell in it" (Psa. 24:1; cp. Psa. 50:12b; 1 Cor. 10:26). Therefore the faithful must declare the quite logical political reality: "You are the God, You alone, of *all the kingdoms* of the earth. You have made heaven and earth" (2 Kgs. 19:15b; cp. Neh. 9:6a; Rev. 4:11a).

We see this powerful truth declared to mighty Nebuchadnezzar, king of the Babylonian empire. Daniel informs him that it is God "who changes the times and the epochs; / He removes kings and establishes kings" (Dan. 2:21a). Daniel reiterates this later when he declares: "that the Most High is ruler over the realm of mankind, / And bestows it on whom He wishes" (Dan. 4:17a).

Truly we must recognize God as the Lord of all, for he is "the blessed and only Sovereign, the King of kings and Lord of lords" (1 Tim. 6:15; cp. Deut. 10:17; Psa. 136:3). What is more, in his sovereign administration of world affairs — through his general providence and by his redemptive grace — he has appointed his Son, Jesus Christ, as the "King of kings and Lord of lords" (Rev. 19:16; cp. 17:14). God the Father did this:

> "when He raised [Jesus] from the dead and seated Him at His right hand in the heavenly places, far above all rule and authority and power and dominion, and every name that is named, not only in this age but also in the one to come. And He put all things in subjection under His feet, and gave Him as head over all things to the church." (Eph. 1:20–22)

In fact, "God highly exalted Him, and bestowed on Him the name which is above every name, so that at the name of Jesus every knee will bow, of those who are in heaven and on earth and under the earth" (Phil. 2:9–10; cp. Rom. 14:11; Col. 2:10). Thus, as we have seen, Christ himself claims "all authority in heaven and on earth" has been given to him (Matt. 28:18; cp. Matt. 11:27; 26:64; John 3:35; 13:3; 17:2; 1 Pet. 3:22).

Clearly, in that God created this world, owns everything in it, and possess all authority over it, he is necessarily the ultimate source of all authority. No majestic king or mighty nation can make a claim to unlimited authority. In his governing the world, God is the one who delegates appropriate levels of authority to men. As Jesus informs the representative of mighty Rome, the procurator Pontius Pilate: "You would have no authority over Me, unless it had been given you from above" (John 19:11a). Paul emphasizes this principle to the Christians at Rome, the capital of the Roman empire: "there is no authority except from God, and those which exist are established by God" (Rom. 13:1b).

By the very nature of the case, human governments must be limited in their power. for God is the ultimate power. We may discern this limitation of authority also from another angle, as we note:

### The problem for authority

Limited government is not only demanded because of the glorious nature of our Creator Lord and the subordinate nature of our created world, but because of the fallen nature of our own sinful souls. As Paul informs us: "there is *none* righteous, *not even one*" for "all have sinned and fall short of the glory of God" (Rom. 3:10, 23). The very opening chapters of the Bible trace the origin of sin back to Adam and Eve at the very beginning of the human race (Gen. 3:1–19).[1] Sin originally arose in the human race with the consequence that "through one man sin entered into the world, and death through sin, and so death spread to *all men*" (Rom. 5:12).

Though God gave government for our good (Rom. 13:1–4; 1 Pet. 2:13–14), we *and our governing authorities* are not good. Jeremiah well captures the problem of sin when he declares "The heart is more deceitful than all else / And is desperately sick; / Who can understand it?" (Jer. 17:9). How could men with such hearts be given unlimited authority over the lives of the nation? Because of sin, governmental power must be constrained.

But now we must note:

### The limits on authority

*The Old Testament law.* Before Israel enters the Promised Land and before she has a king, God warns her about her future desire for a king. In Deuteronomy 17:14–20 he reveals what we know as "the law of the king." In this law we see God imposing limitations on the king, as we shall see.

---

[1] See also: Job 31:33; Hos. 6:7; Rom. 5:12–14; 1 Cor. 15:22; 1 Tim. 2:13–14.

Before we analyze this important passage, we must understand that though Israel stood in a special relationship with God, she was not to live only for herself. She was to be a "kingdom of priests" (Exo. 19:6; cp. Isa. 61:6) so that she might take God's message to the world. Thus, she received her law which was to be a righteous pattern for the nations of the world (Deut. 4:6). Because of all of this, we can discern principles regarding the proper conduct of government from "law of the king" revelation in Deuteronomy 17. That passage reads:

> "When you enter the land which the LORD your God gives you, and you possess it and live in it, and you say, 'I will set a king over me like all the nations who are around me,' you shall surely set a king over you whom the LORD your God chooses, one from among your countrymen you shall set as king over yourselves; you may not put a foreigner over yourselves who is not your countryman. Moreover, he shall not multiply horses for himself, nor shall he cause the people to return to Egypt to multiply horses, since the LORD has said to you, 'You shall never again return that way.' He shall not multiply wives for himself, or else his heart will turn away; nor shall he greatly increase silver and gold for himself. Now it shall come about when he sits on the throne of his kingdom, he shall write for himself a copy of this law on a scroll in the presence of the Levitical priests. It shall be with him and he shall read it all the days of his life, that he may learn to fear the LORD his God, by carefully observing all the words of this law and these statutes, that his heart may not be lifted up above his countrymen and that he may not turn aside from the commandment, to the right or the left, so that he and his sons may continue long in his kingdom in the midst of Israel." (Deut. 17:14–20)

Here we see several limitations placed on the power of the king and his government. First, God commands the king that "he shall not multiply horses for himself . . . nor shall he greatly increase silver and gold for himself" (Deut. 17:16–17). Why does God constrain these particular items? What do they represent? The silver and gold obviously represents monetary wealth. But what about the horses? And why is the king forbidden the abundance of both of these things?

Horses were significant in antiquity in that they were expensive; riding a horse was a sign of wealth and power in the Ancient Near East. Because of their association with wealth, Solomon could relate an ironic turn of events in Ecclesiastes 10:7: "I have seen slaves riding on horses and princes walking like slaves on the land."

In Isaiah God denounces rebellious Israel for her sin and her succumbing to "influences from the east" (Isa. 2:6). He then immediately mentions their ostentatious displays of wealth by his statement which poetically parallels endless treasures with numerous horses. This Hebraic paralleling presents horses as a sign of wealth:

"Their land has also been filled with silver and gold
And there is no end to their treasures;
Their land has also been filled with horses
And there is no end to their chariots." (Isa. 2:7)

In addition, Ezekiel observes that wealthy Assyrian nobles were known for their purple robes and horsemen and horses (Eze. 23:6, 23).

So what? The point we must understand from the law of the king is this: kings are not to inordinately multiply their government's *wealth*. Why? Because they can only do so by excessive taxation and intrusion into the lives of the people. The wealth of a king is gotten from his citizens, not through mutually-beneficial, voluntary transactions in a free market. History teaches that "a rich state means a poor people."[2]

We see a prediction of the breach of the law of the king in 1 Samuel 8, where Israel actually does begin to ask for their first king. There we discover that Samuel is angry with Israel for desiring a king (1 Sam. 8:4–6). He warns her:

"This will be the procedure of the king who will reign over you: he will take your sons and place them for himself in his chariots and among his horsemen and they will run before his chariots. He will appoint for himself commanders of thousands and of fifties, and some to do his plowing and to reap his harvest and to make his weapons of war and equipment for his chariots. He will also take your daughters for perfumers and cooks and bakers. He will take the best of your fields and your vineyards and your olive groves and give them to his servants. He will take a tenth of your seed and of your vineyards and give to his officers and to his servants. He will also take your male servants and your female servants and your best young men and your donkeys and use them for his work. He will take a tenth of your flocks, and you yourselves will become his servants. Then you will cry out in that day because of

---

[2] Rousas J. Rushdoony, *The Institutes of Biblical Law* (Phillipsburg, N. J.: Craig, 1973), 217.

your king whom you have chosen for yourselves, but the LORD will not answer you in that day." (1 Sam. 8:11–18)

Here we see how burdensome Israel's king will become. He will exercise far-reaching power that will dominate their lives, control much of the economy, and burden them with excessive taxes (a "tenth"!). He will do this despite the limits God's law placed on him in Deuteronomy 17 (and elsewhere).

Second, the king may not "cause the people to return to Egypt" nor shall he "multiply wives for himself" (Deut. 17:16, 17). Egypt, of course, was the "house of bondage" for Israel (Exo. 13:3; 20:2; Deut. 7:8). And the reference to "multiplying wives" refers to a practice in antiquity whereby kings made treaties with other nations by marrying the daughters of those foreign kings. King Solomon of Israel did this very thing: "Solomon formed a marriage alliance with Pharaoh king of Egypt, and took Pharaoh's daughter and brought her to the city of David" (1 Kgs. 3:1a).

Here the law of the king is warning against Israel's future king leading the people back into Egyptian-bondage and is discouraging him from establishing entangling alliances with her former slave-master. Israel's experience in Egypt was one of slavery to a dominating government: Pharaoh "appointed taskmasters over them to afflict them with hard labor. And they built for Pharaoh storage cities, Pithom and Raamses" (Exo. 1:11). The unlimited state is an enslaving state. The law of the king warns the king not to erect such a government.

Third, the law of the king then requires of the king that:

> "when he sits on the throne of his kingdom, he shall write for himself a copy of this law on a scroll in the presence of the Levitical priests. It shall be with him and he shall read it all the days of his life, that he may learn to fear the LORD his God, by carefully observing all the words of this law and these statutes, that his heart may not be lifted up above his countrymen and that he may not turn aside from the commandment, to the right or the left, so that he and his sons may continue long in his kingdom in the midst of Israel." (Deut. 17:18–20)

The king's power here is once again limited; here in two important ways. God's covenantal law is Israel's "constitution." Her future king is required to know and abide by her constitution — always. This is so important a limitation on him that he must have an approved, properly-witnessed, and authenticated copy of the law ("constitution"). In Israel this would be overseen by the Levitical priests. This was to insure that he had a clear understanding of the exact law that governs him and the land. It must be with him "all the days of his life."

Not only so but "when he sits on the throne of his kingdom" he must govern "by carefully observing all the words of this law and these statutes." He "may not turn aside from the commandment, to the right or the left." This demands what we call today a "strict construction "of Israel's constitution. See my discussion of this matter in chapter 4 above. And a strict construction of the U. S. Constitution imposes limits on governmental authority (see below).

Simply put: the law of the king limits the power of government. It requires that the political leader of a nation must operate within the limits of the nation's constitution properly understood and applied.

*The New Testament principle.* When we come to the New Testament we see principles continuing the concept of limited government. In Matthew 22 Jesus effectively rebukes Rome's imposition of unlimited power when he responds to the question of the poll-tax to Caesar.

> "'Tell us then, what do You think? Is it lawful to give a poll-tax to Caesar, or not?' But Jesus perceived their malice, and said, 'Why are you testing Me, you hypocrites? Show Me the coin used for the poll-tax.' And they brought Him a denarius. And He said to them, 'Whose likeness and inscription is this?' They said to Him, 'Caesar's.' Then He said to them, 'Then render to Caesar the things that are Caesar's; and to God the things that are God's.'"

The coin brought to Jesus was a Roman denarius from the emperor Tiberius. This coin "would carry his garlanded portrait surrounded by the inscription 'Ti[berius] Caesar Divi Aug[gusti] F]ilius] Augustus'"; on the reverse would be 'Pontif[ex] Maxim[us].' He is thus proclaimed to be not only son of the divine Augustus, but also a high priest" in the imperial cult.[3] Caesar, the civil ruler, has a legitimate right to collect taxes, says Jesus. But he has no right to seek divine worship. His power is limited; the state may not act as god, controlling all. See my discussion in chapter 2 above regarding the statist claim to god-like authority.

---

[3] R. T. France, *The Gospel of Matthew* (NICNT) (Grand Rapids: Eerdmans, 2007), 833.

In Romans we discover another confirmation of the limits of governmental authority. There Paul requires that "every person is to be in subjection to the governing authorities" because they are "established by God" (Rom. 13:1) by "the ordinance of God (Rom. 13:2). This discourages an unlimited governmental authority because Paul also teaches that the ruler "is a minister of God," a "servant of God" (Rom. 13:4, 6). We are only to "render to all what is due them" (Rom. 13:7). Once again we see that the civil magistrate is under God's authority; they are not given civil authority carte blanche.

*The New Testament practice.* Though Peter commands submission to rightful governmental authority (1 Pet. 2:13–15; cp. Rom. 13:1–4), he did not see this as demanding a total submission to a government claiming unlimited power.

In Acts 5:27 Peter and the apostles were commanded by the Jerusalem authorities (the Council) which included the high priest, to "not to continue teaching in this name," i.e., Jesus' name. The high priest and Sanhedrin represented an appropriate governmental authority in Jerusalem, for later when Paul accidentally rebuked the high priest because he did not recognize who he was, he apologized, citing Scripture and explaining that "you shall not speak evil of a ruler of your people" (Acts 23:5).

Despite the legitimate government in Jerusalem, in Acts 5:29 Peter denied the Council's unlimited authority by declaring: "we must obey God rather than men." He is operating under the notion of limited governmental power.

## Constitutional Law

Our Constitution was established within a Christian context under the principled conviction of limited government. Our forefathers held that liberties are God-created, not state-created. They separated from England by rejecting the king's assertion of virtually unlimited power of the colonies. The forerunner and foundation to our Constitution was the Declaration of Independence. It opens with these powerful and important words:

> "When in the Course of human events, it becomes necessary for one people to dissolve the political bands which have connected them with another, and to assume among the powers of the earth, the separate and equal station to which the Laws of Nature and of Nature's God entitle

them, a decent respect to the opinions of mankind requires that they should declare the causes which impel them to the separation.

"We hold these truths to be self-evident, that all men are created equal, that they are endowed by their Creator with certain unalienable Rights, that among these are Life, Liberty and the pursuit of Happiness. — That to secure these rights, Governments are instituted among Men, deriving their just powers from the consent of the governed, — That whenever any Form of Government becomes destructive of these ends, it is the Right of the People to alter or to abolish it, and to institute new Government, laying its foundation on such principles and organizing its powers in such form, as to them shall seem most likely to effect their Safety and Happiness. . . .

"But when a long train of abuses and usurpations, pursuing invariably the same Object evinces a design to reduce them under absolute Despotism, it is their right, it is their duty, to throw off such Government, and to provide new Guards for their future security.--Such has been the patient sufferance of these Colonies; and such is now the necessity which constrains them to alter their former Systems of Government. The history of the present King of Great Britain is a history of repeated injuries and usurpations, all having in direct object the establishment of an absolute Tyranny over these States."

After listing one abuse of power after another by King George III, the Declaration ends with these words:

"In every stage of these Oppressions We have Petitioned for Redress in the most humble terms: Our repeated Petitions have been answered only by repeated injury. A Prince whose character is thus marked by every act which may define a Tyrant, is unfit to be the ruler of a free people. . . .

"We, therefore, the Representatives of the united States of America, in General Congress, Assembled, appealing to the Supreme Judge of the world for the rectitude of our intentions, do, in the Name, and by Authority of the good People of these Colonies, solemnly publish and declare, That these United Colonies are, and of Right ought to be Free and Independent States; that they are Absolved from all Allegiance to the British Crown, and that all political connection between them and the State of Great Britain, is and ought to be totally dissolved; and that as Free and Independent States, they have full Power to levy War, conclude Peace, contract Alliances, establish Commerce, and to do all other Acts and Things which Independent States may of right do. And for the support of this Declaration, with a firm reliance on the protection of divine Providence, we mutually pledge to each other our Lives, our Fortunes and our sacred Honor."

Clearly then, we see that our Christian forefathers called upon God to recognize "the rectitude of our intentions" and they proceeded with "a firm reliance on the protection of divine Providence." They rejected the oppression of King George III and sought to establish a new and limited state.

Just a few years later our Constitution was adopted, continuing the desire for limited government. Because of the concerns for a constrained governmental power, our Constitution established a political structure that divided federal power into branches (diffused powers), with each given specific responsibilities (express powers) so that no branch has more power than the other branches (balanced powers).

I will consider limited government in terms of these three principles which comport well with a biblical view of government. Christian citizens need to recognize how biblical principles of limited government are embodied in our own Constitution.

## Diffused power

Our nation was born out of the rejection of a king whose power had become so concentrated and powerful as to be intolerable. Consequently, our Constitution established a limited government of *diffused power*. That is, the authority of our government was distributed over three branches of the federal government at the national level — and dispersed among several layers of lower governments. As a consequence, our Constitutional form of government heeds a warning made famous later by Lord Acton: "power tends to corrupt and absolute power corrupts absolutely."

In America governmental power is limited by means of its being distributed rather than concentrated. The very separation of powers in our Constitution was designed for the purpose of diffusing power. On the federal level we have three branches of government, the executive (the president), legislative (Congress), and judicial (Supreme Court). Thus, the three powers of government — executive, legislative, judicial powers — are separated. Power is not concentrated into the hands of one man or even one group of men.

Article 1, section 1 of the Constitution declares that "All legislative Powers herein granted shall be vested in a Congress of the United States, which shall consist of a Senate and House of Representatives."

Article 2, section 1 reads: "The executive Power shall be vested in a President of the United States of America." Article 3, section 1 reads: "The judicial Power of the United States shall be vested in one supreme Court, and in such inferior Courts as the Congress may from time to time ordain and establish."

But this is not even the full story of the diffusion of power. Two of the three branches of government involve election to office. Regarding the legislative branch, Article 1, section 2 states that: "The House of Representatives shall be composed of Members chosen every second Year by the People of the several States." The original, unamended Constitution established a different method for electing Senators than we now practice. Article 1, section 3 declared that "the Senate of the United States shall be composed of two Senators from each State, chosen by the Legislature thereof for six Years." This diffused the power of the federal government by having the state legislatures appoint Senators. Of course, the state legislatures were elected by popular vote. Senatorial elections, however, eventually shifted from state legislative action to direct popular vote by the Seventeenth Amendment (1913).

The president is also an elected office, of course. He is elected indirectly by means of electors in the Electoral College. Article 2, section 1 of the Constitution states: "Each State shall appoint, in such Manner as the Legislature thereof may direct, a Number of Electors, equal to the whole Number of Senators and Representatives to which the State may be entitled in the Congress." But again, since the legislatures are popularly elected, this involves an indirect popular vote for the presidency.

The federal power is even further diffused by the division of the legislative branch into two houses, the Senate and House of Representatives, as per Article 1, section 1. Each of these houses have many "members" plural, further dispersing power (Art. 1, sect. 2; cp. Art. 2, sect. 3).

And the power of each house is limited even more in that their members serve limited terms, whereupon they must run again in order to be re-elected. Congressmen are elected for two year terms (Art. 1, sect. 2), Senators for six year terms (Art. 1, sect. 3). The president serves a term of four years (Art. 2, sect. 1), and in the Twenty-second Amendment, he was limited to serving only ten years total (ratified 1951).

Still further diffusion of power is established by the fact that the nation is composed of several states who are granted various powers. For instance, each state is represented in the federal government by Congressmen and Senators (Art. 1, sect. 1; Art. 2, sect. 2; Amend. 14, sect. 2), the states appoint the electors who elect the president (Art. 2, sect. 1; Amend. 12), the states are guaranteed a "Republican Form of Government" (Art. 4), the Constitution can be amended by action of two-thirds of the states (Art. 5), and so forth. Indeed, the Tenth Amendment insures that: "The powers not delegated to the United States by the Constitution, nor prohibited by it to the States, are reserved to the States respectively, or to the people."

Our Constitution takes seriously the notion of limited government. Sadly today, the growing tendency of politicians and jurists is to view the Constitution as a "living document" constantly accruing new and stronger powers (see discussion in ch. 4).

But not only must we recognize diffused power in our Constitutional system, but also that which results from it:

**Balanced power**

The power of government is not only dispersed power, but *counterbalanced* power. It is not simply a question of a majority vote of all the Congressmen, Senators, Supreme Court justices, and the president, but their offices are intentionally designed to weigh against each other. This further imposes a limitation of power on government — when the Constitution is followed. In the *Federalist #51* James Madison wrote:

> "The great security against a gradual concentration of the several powers in the same department, consists in giving to those who administer each department the necessary constitutional means and personal motives to resist encroachments of the others."

The executive branch of the government is constrained from asserting absolute power by the fact that the legislative branch holds the purse strings of government: "All Bills for raising Revenue shall originate in the House of Representatives" (Art. 1, sect. 7). Thus, the president may attempt by unilateral executive action to engage some action, but Congress alone can fund that action. And though he is the "Commander in Chief" of the national military forces (Art. 2, sect. 2), Congress alone may declare and fund war (Art. 1, sect. 8).

The legislative branch of government may pass laws, but these laws can be vetoed by the president in the executive branch and may be struck down by the Supreme Court in the judicial branch. Article 1, section 7 states regarding the president's power to veto a bill passed by Congress: "If he approve he shall sign it, but if not he shall return it, with his

Objections to that House in which it shall have originated, who shall enter the Objections at large on their Journal, and proceed to reconsider it."

The Supreme Court also may examine and block Congressional legislation: "The judicial Power shall extend to all Cases, in Law and Equity, arising under this Constitution, the Laws of the United States" (Art. 3, sect. 2). This section also requires that Congress must secure a two-thirds vote to override his veto. Furthermore, the necessity of recurring elections counter-balances any run-away Congressional action.

The "Judges of the Supreme Court" are appointed by the president "by and with the Advice and Consent of the Senate" (Art. 2, sect. 2). Congress has power to regulate the Supreme Court: "the Supreme Court shall have appellate Jurisdiction, both as to Law and Fact, with such Exceptions, and under such Regulations as the Congress shall make" (Art. 3, sect. 2).

Furthermore, every officer in each branch of government operates under the possible threat of impeachment, if any offense rises to that level (Art. 1, sect. 2, 3; Art. 2, sect. 2, 4; Art. 3, sect. 1). And each branch is limited in its power by constraints arising from the Bill of Rights.

What is more, the Constitution may be amended by powers outside of the federal government, thereby potentially providing further counter-balancing of federal power:

> "The Congress, whenever two thirds of both Houses shall deem it necessary, shall propose Amendments to this Constitution, or, on the Application of the Legislatures of two thirds of the several States, shall call a Convention for proposing Amendments, which, in either Case, shall be valid to all Intents and Purposes, as Part of this Constitution, when ratified by the Legislatures of three fourths of the several States, or by Conventions in three fourths thereof." (Art. 5)

In all of these strictures regarding the balance of power, we must recognize that even the majority is not given free hand to govern as they please:

> "In many ways the Constitution is designed to frustrate the desire of political majorities to work their will through the exercise of government power: individual, state, federal. The most obvious example of this is the first ten amendments to the Constitution, or the Bill of Rights.

These amendments guarantee certain individual freedoms against political infringement regardless of majority will."[4]

## Expressed power

All of this diffusion into several branches and layers of government and the balancing of power by checks and balances is enhanced by the doctrine of expressed powers. The doctrine of "expressed power" holds that the federal government has only those powers specifically set forth in the Constitution.

We see the expressed-powers doctrine in Article 1, section 8 of the Constitution, for instance. There we read that "the Congress shall have Power to," then it outlines twenty-seven (not 27,000,000!) specific powers in eighteen brief paragraphs. Article 1, section 9 even provides the extra precaution of specifically listing powers Congress does *not* have.

In Article 2, sections 2 and 3 the specific powers of the president are enumerated. There we read: the president "shall be," "shall have Power," "shall appoint," and so forth.

Article 6 speaks of "this Constitution, and the Laws of the United States which shall be made in pursuance thereof." The laws of the land must be in pursuance of the Constitution, and not unrelated to or unwarranted by it.

Amendment 10 of the Bill of Rights makes a clear, powerful, and important statement regarding this expressed-powers doctrine. The federal government has limited powers because "the powers not delegated to the United States by the Constitution, nor prohibited by it to the States, are reserved to the States respectively, or to the people."

## Conclusion

We do not have a perfect Constitution; it is certainly not inspired and inerrant. But we do have a very potent one that was carefully designed to limit the power of the federal government in order to insure our liberties. It arose in a Christian context, one that distrusted governmental power as recently experienced by the American colonies under King George III.

---

[4] Dwight R. Lee, "The Political Economy of the U.S. Constitution," *The Freeman* 37:2 (Feb., 1987). http://www.thefreemanonline.org/columns/the-political-eco nomy-of-the-us-constitution/

Dwight R. Lee notes that: "The genesis of the political and economic wisdom of our Founding Fathers is found in the fact that they distrusted government while fully recognizing the necessity of government for a beneficent social order."[5] Clinton Rossiter even argues that "liberty rather than authority, protection rather than power, delay rather than efficiency were the concern of these constitution-makers."[6]

As Christians we do not believe "In Washington We Trust." Nor do we accept as our pledge: "One Nation Under Washington." Simply put, we do not believe in salvation by politics. Because of our doctrines of an exalted God and fallen man, we recognize the need for limited government.

In fact, we hold that other powers exist than just the state. God has parceled out authority to men in four fundamental spheres of government: personal government (self), family government (home), ecclesiastical government (church), and civil government (state). Three of these spheres overlay the foundational layer of self or personal government and have symbols of their own power: family government has the rod (Prov. 13:24; 22:15; 23:13; 29:15), church government the keys (Matt. 16:19; cp. Isa. 22:22; Rev. 1:18; 3:7), and civil government the sword (Rom. 13:4; cp. Acts 12:2). Civil government is not the only authority under which we live.

As Christians, we should welcome opportunities to participate in government with the goal of influencing the state to conform to God's will for it as a social institution. We believe that "By the blessing of the upright a city is exalted, / But by the mouth of the wicked it is torn down" (Prov. 11:11). Our loyalty to God as the Supreme Authority calls us to political involvement in an effort to maintain a good and just government of limited authority. The involvement of righteous people can significantly influence government for the better.

---

[5] Dwight R. Lee, "The Political Economy of the U. S. Constitution,"

[6] Clinton Rossiter, *Seedtime of the Republic: The Origin of the American Tradition of Political Liberty* (New York: Harcourt. Brace and World. 1953), 425.

## Chapter 6

# ECONOMIC FREEDOM

"You shall surely set a king over you whom the LORD your God chooses. . . . He shall not multiply horses for himself . . . nor shall he greatly increase silver and gold for himself." (Deut. 17:15–17)

## Introduction

Most people deem economics to be boring and therefore have little interest in it. It is not known as the "dismal science" for no reason. Yet we make economic decisions every single day of our lives. Basically, economics may be reduced to the problem of balancing scarcity and choices. Thus, on the personal level economics involves our trying to balance scarce resources (time, property, and money) with infinite desires.

We make an economic decision, for instance, when we choose either to relax at home or to go shopping or to work more to gain extra money. Each of these optional actions makes a different economic impact on our wealth. We see this economic struggle constantly at work in our lives: We decide to buy one thing rather than another; we consider saving money for the future or spending it now; we determine to pay for something outright or charge it. We seek jobs that pay a certain wage, we pay taxes when we buy something, we put aside money for retirement, and we save for vacations. On and on we could go listing the practical, everyday decisions we face that are impacted by economic considerations.

Thus, economics takes on God-like dimensions in that it is an omnipresent, all powerful, and perpetual concern for us. Consequently, in this book on politics I must touch on economic issues from a Christian worldview perspective. In order to demonstrate the relevance of economics in the political debate, I will begin by highlighting:

## Our National Problem

The economic reality of scarcity holds true on both the personal level for individuals as well as on the national level for governments. Unfortunately, as economist Thomas Sowell observes:

"The first lesson of economics is scarcity: There is never enough of anything to satisfy all those who want it. The first lesson of politics is to disregard the first lesson of economics."[1]

Because of this failure of government to recognize the most basic principle of economics, this issue is a huge concern in politics since government spends enormous amounts of money — *our* money. It invests billions of dollars in defending our nation, building our roads, policing our streets, maintaining our courts, punishing our criminals, regulating our economy, engaging in research, funding our schools, managing our social programs, paying interest on its debt, and much, much, much, much, much, much, much, much more.

The following federal government figures are from the fiscal year 2011. The government's total debt in that year was $15.5 trillion. This debt represents 102% of the Gross Domestic Product (the market value of all goods and services produced within a given period). This debt amounts to $49,225 per American citizen. The deficit (the amount of expenditures exceeding income) was $1.3 trillion. The interest cost on the federal government debt was $454.4 billion.[2]

Despite this ever-deepening debt crisis, Thomas Sowell notes that:

"Most of us might be a little skittish about spending money if we were teetering on the brink of bankruptcy. But the beauty of being a politician is that it is all other people's money, including among those other people generations yet unborn."[3]

To make matters worse, most citizens do not fully grasp the fact that the federal government only has money that it either takes from us through taxation or it steals from us through inflation. We tend to vote as if money can be created out of thin air.

As worldview-oriented Christians we must recognize the biblical foundations for a proper economics. It is too easy to get swept away by the rhetoric that so readily flows all around us. In early colonial America the Bible was the textbook for life. As I noted in chapter 2 above, it even

---

[1] http://jpetrie.myweb.uga.edu/sowell.html

[2] http://www.usgovernmentspending.com/spending_chart_1950_2015USp_H0t%22

[3] Thomas Sowell, "Getting Nowhere, Fast" *National Review Online* (Feb. 1, 2012). http://www.nationalreview.com/author/200445/latest

powerfully influenced law and politics among our forefathers. And this is the way it should be, for Paul claims the Bible *is* a textbook for *all* of life: "All Scripture is inspired by God and *profitable* for teaching, for reproof, for correction, for training in righteousness; so that the man of God may be *adequate, equipped for every good work*" (2 Tim. 3:16–17).

As God's divinely-revealed interpretation of all of life equipping us for "every good work," the Bible is also a textbook for economics. Of course, it does not provide formal, scientific, textbook-like analyses of the principles or statistics of production, distribution, and consumption of goods and services. If it did, it would be even *less* read than it is! But it does establish basic principles and provide key insights into foundational economic issues.

So let us consider some of the very basic principles that the Bible establishes regarding economics. I will begin by briefly considering:

### The Bible and Economic Dangers

Though the Bible is not a formal textbook on economics, it nevertheless is filled with economic insights. These insights appear repeatedly in God's law as it establishes economic rights, frequently in the prophets as they denounce economic sins, often in Jesus' parables as he illustrates spiritual truths by economic realities, and much in the teachings of the Apostles as they confront economic abuses. Clearly economic issues are not some sparsely discussed topic in Scripture.

As we get started with the dangers inherent in economics, once again we must return to:

### The problem of sin

Sin is a universal phenomenon that leads to universal woes. The Bible repeatedly teaches that all men are fallen creatures and prone to evil. Paul puts the matter concisely when he writes: "for all have sinned and fall short of the glory of God" (Rom. 3:23).

As I noted in earlier chapters, the sin problem has a large place in the Christian worldview (ch. 1), explains our moral situation (ch. 3), led our forefathers to establish a nation constrained by a Constitution (ch. 4) which imposed limited government with checks-and-balances (ch. 5). However, the sin problem will not go away — despite limitations on government. The citizenry as well as the government are sinners. Even the votes of a free electorate are affected by sin. And this causes economic dangers. Let me explain.

Almost certainly the most prevalent sin among men is an economic sin: covetousness. And this universal sin is exacerbated by the fundamental economic reality that we face: scarcity. Scarcity encourages coveting, as we desire those things we cannot easily have. Comedian Steven Wright dismisses this sin more easily than most with his jocular logic: "You can't have everything. Where would you put it?"

Covetousness is such a potent sin that God specifically prohibits it in the summary of his law, the Ten Commandments. Jesus lists it in his brief catalog of sins that proceed out of the heart and corrupt a man (Mark 7:21–23). Apparently this was the sin that led the rich young ruler away from Jesus: he claims to have kept all the commandments Jesus named — but Jesus omitted covetousness so that he could challenge him on that point (Mark 10:17–22).

The Apostle Paul lists covetousness in his greatly abbreviated summary of the Ten Commandments (Rom. 13:9). He even confesses and laments his own tendency to this sin when he writes: "Sin, taking opportunity through the commandment, produced in me coveting of every kind" (Rom. 7:8). For Paul covetousness is tantamount to idolatry: "For this you know with certainty, that no immoral or impure person or *covetous man, who is an idolate*r, has an inheritance in the kingdom of Christ and God" (Eph. 5:5). Therefore, he too lists covetousness in his catalogs of sin (Rom. 13:9; 1 Cor. 5:10–11; 6:9–10).

The universal draw of covetousness often leads to the destructive sin of envy. Though both envy and jealousy can arise within the context of covetousness, envy is worse than jealousy. Jealousy can be either good or bad ("God is a jealous God," Exo. 20:5; 34:14; Deut. 5:9); it is basically a desire for something. But envy is always an evil, appearing repeatedly in the several New Testament catalogs of evil (Mark 7:22; Rom. 1:29; Gal. 5:21; 1 Tim. 6:4; Tit. 3:3; 1 Pet. 2:1). Envy goes beyond sinful jealousy. Whereas the jealous person wants something for himself, the envious one simply wants the other person to not have something – whether or not the envious person himself wants it. Envy wishes misfortune on its object.

Covetousness fueled by envy is a very real economic danger today. It is stirring up the class resentment that we are witnessing all around us — as we saw in the Occupy Wall Street movement. This class warfare is being encouraged by liberal politicians, tenured academics, big-media pundits, and others. They claim to stand for the 99% of our citizens who are supposedly dominated by the 1% who are wealthy. This only aggravates our serious economic problems, and in no one helps us alleviate them.

Since most Americans have little understanding of economics, and since covetousness is a powerful sin, government becomes for voters the illusion that we can all live off somebody else. It re-formulates the eighth commandment to read: "Thou shalt not steal, except by majority vote." Because of covetousness and envy, as the old joke goes, our democratic system becomes a voting arrangement whereby two wolves and a sheep vote on what to have for dinner.

We daily witness in the papers the vitriol being poured upon our historic free-market economic system which made us the most prosperous nation in history. The successful, job-producing businessmen of America are particularly denounced for not paying their "fair share" in taxes, for their "obscene profits," for being "greedy capitalist 1 percenters," for being "selfish," and more.

Blame-the-rich/soak-the-rich rhetoric echoes through the streets and in the hollow heads of the pundits. And it does so while our federal government's largesse is re-distributing our wealth by out-of-control entitlements and increasing our indebtedness by ever-growing deficits.

This anger over great disparities in wealth distribution in our nation is greatly exacerbated by unfamiliarity with the facts. For instance, let us consider the reality of wealth distribution in America:

> "The Treasury Department's latest study on income mobility in America found that during the 10-year period starting in 1996, roughly half of the taxpayers who started in the bottom 20 percent had moved up to a higher income group by 2005."[4]

In fact, their incomes increased by 91 percent while those taxpayers in the top 20 percent witnessed only a 10 percent increase in the same time period. Those in the top 5 percent even saw their income decline.[5]

---

[4] Paul Ryan, "How Class Warfare Weakens America," *New York Post* (Oct. 27, 2011). He is referencing the U. S. Department of the Treasury, "Income Mobility in the U.S. from 1996 to 2005 (Nov. 13, 2007). http://www.nypost.com/ p/news/ opinion/opedcolumnists/how_class_warfare_weakens_america_2RiwAsufcsk9u lnS7xJBlK

[5] "Movin' On Up," *Wall Street Journal* (Nov. 13, 2007), A25.

Through a clever statistics-denying sleight-of-hand, the debate has been framed in terms of wealth differences between *people*. But economist Thomas Sowell explains the reality of wealth disparities in our productive, economically-mobile society:

> "Although such discussions have been phrased in terms of *people,* the actual empirical evidence cited has been about what has been happening over time to *statistical categories* — and that turns out to be the direct opposite of what has happened over time to flesh-and-blood human beings, most of whom *move* from one income category to another over time. . . . It is not the same individuals in the same categories over the years."

The complaints protesting economic disparities hinder our free-market system, which actually helps people to rise up the economic ladder. Not only so but it establishes a dangerous pattern that overwhelms our Constitutional checks-and-balances. And in doing so, the complainants demand proposals that go against biblical law. How so?

In biblical law, justice must be *blind*. It must be unbiased toward *any* person or class of people. Even the half shekel tax for God's sanctuary for worship was to be made equally by all: "The rich shall not pay more and the poor shall not pay less than the half shekel" (Exo. 30:15a). So it is not surprising that in the broader civil society God also commands: "You shall do no injustice in judgment; you shall not be partial to the poor nor defer to the great, but you are to judge your neighbor fairly" (Lev. 19:15). God warns: "Nor shall you be partial to a poor man in his dispute" (Exo. 23:3; cp. Deut. 1:17; 10:17; 16:19).

Covetousness in a democratic economy generates policies and laws that reduce economic growth for the nation and hinder economic advancement for individuals.

### The problem of indebtedness

As we have seen in our brief notes above, and as we are well aware from current news items, our federal government has piled up enormous debt. In fact, our debt has gotten so bad that for the first time since credit agencies began rating debt (beginning in 1917) our national credit rating was downgraded in 2011.[6]

What is more, this is no temporary hump in the road for our economic well-being. Our national debt is neither shrinking nor holding steady, but is skyrocketing. From 2008 to 2011 — a period covering just five years — our debt has increased by over 50%. Note the growth of our debt in the following federal years[7]:

FY 2008: $10.0 trillion
FY 2009: $11.9 trillion
FY 2010: $13.5 trillion
FY 2011: $15.5 trillion
FY 2012: $16.7 trillion

But matters are even worse than they first appear; this is only the tip of iceberg. In fact, the iceberg we are seeing is more like Antarctica. Economist Walter E. Williams warns:

> "Federal 2010 Medicare and Medicaid expenditures totaled $800 billion. The projected annual growth of both programs is about 7 percent. Social Security expenditures are more than $700 billion a year. According to the 2009 Social Security and Medicare trustees reports, by 2030, 49 percent of federal revenues will go for Social Security and Medicare payments. The unfunded liability of both programs is already $106 trillion."[8]

We are no longer talking chump change of just a few trillion dollars.

Because of creeping socialism in America and our sense of economic entitlement, we keep voting in politicians who promise us more of this and more of that. This inexorably leads us ever more deeply into excessive indebtedness. We are proving the reality of *The Devil Dictionary's* definition of "vote": "the instrument and symbol of a freeman's power to make a fool of himself and a wreck of his country." As our excessive indebtedness shows, "Socialism is a philosophy of failure, the creed of

---

[6] "S&P, in historical move, downgrades U.S. credit rating," *Xinhuanet.com* (Aug., 6, 2011). http://news.xinhuanet.com/english2010/business/2011-08/06/c_131032871.htm

[7] See: http://www.usgovernmentdebt.us/

[8] Walter E. Williams, "Economic Chaos Ahead," *Townhall.com* (Feb. 8, 2012). http://townhall.com/columnists/walterewilliams/2012/02/08/economic_chaos_ahead

ignorance, and the gospel of envy, its inherent virtue is the equal sharing of misery" (Winston Churchill).

Biblical economics discourages indebtedness by warning that "the borrower becomes the lender's slave" (Prov. 22:7b). In a parallelism in Deuteronomy 15:6b we see this discouraging of debt as an instrument of slavery:

> "You will lend to many nations, but you will not borrow; and
> you will rule over many nations, but they will not rule over you."

To borrow is to be ruled over by whoever holds your debt receipt. Those who are indebted are also deemed the tail rather than the head because of their reduced status. In the covenantal warning of curses to befall Israel if she breaks God's law, we read: "He shall lend to you, but you will not lend to him; he shall be the head, and you will be the tail" (Deut. 28:44).

This slave imagery flows right out of the experience of some who became excessively indebted in Scripture. They had to sell themselves into servitude (basically, indentured servitude). God's law speaks of a those who become so poor that they must sell themselves to another (Lev. 25:39; Deut. 15:12–13). Undoubtedly, many of these became poor by over-reaching and incurring debilitating debt.

As a general principle, Scripture warns that debt brings one to ruin. "Do not be among those who give pledges, / Among those who become guarantors for debts. / If you have nothing with which to pay, / Why should he take your bed from under you?" (Prov. 22:26). Jesus presents a parable wherein one slave owed money to another and was therefore subjected to a beating and imprisonment (Matt. 18:28–30).

God promises Israel that if she follows his law (including the exercise of blind justice) and conducts her national affairs righteously, she will be prosperous and not be a debtor-nation: "The LORD will open for you His good storehouse, the heavens, to give rain to your land in its season and to bless all the work of your hand; and you shall lend to many nations, but you shall not borrow" (Deut. 28:12; cp. 15:6).

A general principle of Christian living is to "owe nothing to anyone" (Rom. 13:8). We should strive for the same principle in government. Unfortunately, a womb-to-tomb governmental policy encourages national debt. Too many Americans today do not see the danger of our out-of-control spending, much of it due to excessive entitlements. We are led to believe: "In Washington We Trust" as we hear the federal government promising: "Come unto me all ye that labor, and I will give you rest." We are learning the reality of Milton Friedman's observation: "If you pay people to be poor you will never run out of poor people."

Because of this, the New Twenty-third Psalm captures the growing national sentiment:

The government is my shepherd:
I need not work.
It alloweth me to lie down on a good job;
It leadeth me beside still factories;
It destroyeth my initiative.
It leadeth me in the path of parasites for politic's sake;

Yea, though I walk through the valley of the shadow of deficits,
I will fear no evil, for the government is with me.
It's entitlements and spending, they comfort me
It prepareth a Utopia for me on the backs of my grandchildren.
It filleth my head with false security;
My inefficiency runneth over.
Surely the government shall care for me all the days of my life,
And I shall dwell in a fool's paradise forever.

## The problem of excessive taxation

We hear a lot of heated debate and high-flying rhetoric about taxes today. The tragedy is that because of excessive government spending and indebtedness, we have to pay high taxes.

It is hard to believe America was founded to avoid high taxation. Economist Walter E. Williams tells an amusing story of an American economist at an economics seminar in England. The British economist friend asked the American where he lived. The American grinned and said: "In Valley Forge, where we put you Britishers to route." The Brit responded: "What was that war all about?" The American proudly replied: "Taxation without representation." To which the Brit asked: "How do you like taxation *with* representation?"

All of us are aware of our income taxes[9] and sales taxes on point-of-sale purchases. Unfortunately though, most of our taxes are hidden so that we pay them unknowingly:

> "Plenty of unexpected taxes raise the price of goods and services: so-called sin taxes, import duties, user fees and excise taxes on things as varied as gas guzzlers, firearms, communications services and air travel.
> "'Most of the hidden taxes pertain to products we buy rather than wages we earn,' says Pete Sepp, executive vice president for the National Taxpayers Union, a watchdog group in Washington, D.C."[10]

And these formal taxes do not reflect the even more hidden "taxes" such as the costs of government regulation of industry[11] or money lost to inflation through government monetary policy. Sadly, Congress' attitude toward hidden taxes is not to do away with them, but to attempt to hide them better.

But once again we can look to Scripture for insights. Though as citizens we are to submit to government taxation: "render to all what is due them: tax to whom tax is due" (Rom. 13:6–7; cp. Matt. 22:17–21), the Bible warns us about the dangers of excessive taxation.

Once again we need to return to Deuteronomy 17 and the law of the king. Deuteronomy was given to Israel in preparation for her entering the Promised Land and taking up her national status (Deut. 1:8, 19–21; 3:28; cp. Josh. 3:17; 4:1). This law warns her against any future desire for a king who spends too much:

> "You shall surely set a king over you whom the LORD your God chooses.
> . . . He shall not multiply horses for himself . . . . He shall not multiply

---

[9] Since the Sixteenth Amendment to the Constitution in 1913, however, our income taxes are incrementally sneaked out of our regular paychecks so that we do not really see them.

[10] "Hidden taxes you pay every day," Money.MSN.com (Feb 15, 2011). http://money.msn.com/tax-planning/hidden-taxes-you-pay-every-day.aspx

[11] "The Code of Federal Regulations is now over 157,000 pages long. Last year alone, 3,503 new rules went into effect — that's a new regulation every 2 1/2 hours, day and night, seven days a week." C. W. Crews, "Regulation: The Huge, Hidden Tax We Pay for Government," Heartland.org (April 16, 2010). http://heartland.org/policy-documents/regulation-huge-hidden-tax-we-pay-government

wives for himself, or else his heart will turn away; nor shall he greatly increase silver and gold for himself." (Deut. 17:15–17)

Instead he should be one who follows God's law so that "his heart may not be lifted up above his countrymen and that he may not turn aside from the commandment" (Deut. 17:18–20). The natural expectation of a king that exceeds biblical constraints by buying goods (horses) and increasing wealth (silver and gold) for himself is that he will levy a heavy tax burden upon the people.

We see this very problem coming to pass in 1 Samuel 8 when Israel actually does demand that Samuel appoint them a king (1 Sam. 8:5). Godly Samuel was displeased and warned them what they must expect if they have a king "like all the nations" (1 Sam. 8:4). His warning shows the excessive burdens their king would place upon them, including multiplying of government jobs and raising exorbitant taxes — *up to 10%!*

> "So Samuel spoke all the words of the LORD to the people who had asked of him a king. He said, 'This will be the procedure of the king who will reign over you: he will take your sons and place them for himself in his chariots and among his horsemen and they will run before his chariots. He will appoint for himself commanders of thousands and of fifties, and some to do his plowing and to reap his harvest and to make his weapons of war and equipment for his chariots. He will also take your daughters for perfumers and cooks and bakers. He will take the best of your fields and your vineyards and your olive groves and give them to his servants. He will take a tenth of your seed and of your vineyards and give to his officers and to his servants. He will also take your male servants and your female servants and your best young men and your donkeys and use them for his work. He will take a tenth of your flocks, and you yourselves will become his servants. Then you will cry out in that day because of your king whom you have chosen for yourselves, but the LORD will not answer you in that day.'" (1 Sam. 8:10–18)

Nehemiah confesses the sins of Israel which led to her exile and domination by a foreign nation. In his confessional prayer he mentioned the Promised Land which was subjected to an oppressive government: "Its abundant produce is for the kings / Whom You have set over us because of our sins; / They also rule over our bodies / And over our cattle as they please, / So we are in great distress" (Neh. 9:37).

Bigger government results in more controls and costs, and therefore more taxes. At the rate we are being taxed today, fears have been expressed that we will soon be receiving a simplified tax form with just two statements: 1. How much money did you make last year? 2. Send it in.

But now we must consider more positively:

## The Bible and Economic Blessings

Our political attitudes and actions should avoid those things that cause national economic disarray, destruction, and despair. Things like engaging in covetousness and envy, increasing national debt, and levying heavy taxes. Rather, we should seek God's wisdom regarding those things that promote our stability, productivity, and sufficiency.

### The blessings of wealth

In Scripture we find that the righteous wealthy are extolled rather than derided. Rather than covetousness and envy controlling the attitudes of God's people toward the successful, honor and admiration for their success should.

Abraham is called "the friend of God (Jms. 2:23; cp. 2 Chron. 20:7; Isa. 41:8). He is called God's servant (Psa. 105:6, 42). He is the Bible's premiere example of faith toward God (Rom. 4:12, 16; Gal. 3:7, 9; Heb. 11:8–19). Yet Abraham was a man of great wealth (Gen. 12:5; 13:6).

Job was a man who "was blameless, upright, fearing God and turning away from evil" (Job 1:1). God greatly commends him: "The LORD said to Satan, 'Have you considered My servant Job? For there is no one like him on the earth, a blameless and upright man, fearing God and turning away from evil" (Job 1:6). God repeats this after Satan afflicts Job: "The LORD said to Satan, 'Have you considered My servant Job? For there is no one like him on the earth, a blameless and upright man fearing God and turning away from evil. And he still holds fast his integrity, although you incited Me against him to ruin him without cause'" (Job 2:3).

Yet in the very context of the first note of praise for Job, we learn that "his possessions also were 7,000 sheep, 3,000 camels, 500 yoke of oxen, 500 female donkeys, and very many servants; and that man was the greatest of all the men of the east" (Job 1:3). Satan even complains of God's favoring Job: "Have You not made a hedge about him and his house and all that he has, on every side? You have blessed the work of his hands, and his possessions have increased in the land" (Job 1:10).

Then at the end of Job's testing we read that God blesses him once again with wealth — even *more* wealth than before: "The LORD restored the fortunes of Job when he prayed for his friends, and the LORD increased all that Job had twofold. . . . The LORD blessed the latter days of Job more than his beginning; and he had 14,000 sheep and 6,000 camels and 1,000 yoke of oxen and 1,000 female donkeys" (Job 42:10, 12).

In the New Testament we read of the wealthy magi bringing expensive gifts to worship Jesus (Matt. 2:1–11). We also learn of the "rich man" Joseph of Arimathea that he came and helped with the body of the crucified Jesus: "When it was evening, there came a rich man from Arimathea, named Joseph, who himself had also become a disciple of Jesus" (Matt. 27:57). Jesus promises his faithful followers: "Everyone who has left houses or brothers or sisters or father or mother or children or farms for My name's sake, will receive many times as much, and will inherit eternal life" (Matt. 19:29). He even speaks a parable comparing the kingdom of heaven to a merchant seeking fine pearls who finds a pearl of great value (Matt. 13:45–46).

We can read of these and other wealthy men whom God commends and blesses. This is as we should expect from the many declarations of God regarding wealth righteously used.

The great blessing-and-curse chapter promises wealth as a blessing to the faithful:

> "The LORD will command the blessing upon you in your barns and in all that you put your hand to, and He will bless you in the land which the LORD your God gives you. The LORD will establish you as a holy people to Himself, as He swore to you, if you keep the commandments of the LORD your God and walk in His ways. . . .The LORD will make you abound in prosperity, in the offspring of your body and in the offspring of your beast and in the produce of your ground, in the land which the LORD swore to your fathers to give you. The LORD will open for you His good storehouse, the heavens, to give rain to your land in its season and to bless all the work of your hand; and you shall lend to many nations, but you shall not borrow. " (Deut. 28:8, 11–12)

Thus, we read in the praise psalms things such as:

> "Praise the LORD! / How blessed is the man who fears the LORD, / Who greatly delights in His commandments. / His descendants will be mighty on earth; / The generation of the upright will be blessed. / Wealth and

riches are in his house, / And his righteousness endures forever." (Psa. 112:1–3)

In the wisdom literature, we see wealth extolled. Proverbs sees wisdom bringing wealth: "Riches and honor are with me, / Enduring wealth and righteousness. . . . To endow those who love me with wealth, / That I may fill their treasuries" (Prov. 8:18, 21). Consequently, we learn that "great wealth is in the house of the righteous" (Prov. 15:6a). Ecclesiastes follows the pattern:

> "Furthermore, as for every man to whom God has given riches and wealth, He has also empowered him to eat from them and to receive his reward and rejoice in his labor; this is the gift of God. For he will not often consider the years of his life, because God keeps him occupied with the gladness of his heart." (Eccl. 5:19–20)

The prophets look to the future of Zion / Jerusalem's blessings, then associate those blessings with wealth. "Your gates will be open continually; / They will not be closed day or night, / So that men may bring to you the wealth of the nations, / With their kings led in procession" (Isa. 60:11). "I will shake all the nations; and they will come with the wealth of all nations, and I will fill this house with glory,' says the LORD of hosts" (Hag. 2:7).

Though Jesus and the Bible condemn living for wealth for its own sake, ill-gotten gains, uncaring use of wealth, and so forth, wealth itself is never deemed an evil. In fact, God even gives wealth to his people as a blessing to confirm his covenant: "you shall remember the LORD your God, for it is He who is giving you power to make wealth, that He may confirm His covenant which He swore to your fathers, as it is this day" (Deut. 8:18).

The shrill denunciations of the wealthy so frequently heard today are unbiblical and unwise. By doing such, society is discouraging productivity. This leads us to note the biblical defense of:

### Private property rights

Wealth is strongly related to property and so naturally leads to our considering the question of private property. In the twentieth century one of the most destructive theories of property arose and caused enormous woes in the world: communism. Though communism is variously explained and was differently applied in the real world, it grew up from the theories of Karl Marx and his opposition to private property.

Thomas Sowell complains: "You might think that the collapse of communism throughout Eastern Europe would be considered a decisive failure for Marxism, but academic Marxists in America are utterly undaunted. . . . Socialism in general has a record of failure so blatant that only an intellectual could ignore or evade it."[12] Marxism remains to this day an influence in some circles of academia, as we can see from Darío Fernández-Morera's book, *American Academia and the Survival of Marxist Ideas* (1996).

In his *Communist Manifesto* Marx wrote: "the theory of the Communists may be summed up in the single sentence: abolition of private property." In 1840 French anarchist Pierre-Joseph Proudhon, a strong influence on Marx, stated in his book *What Is Property?* a famous phrase: "Property is theft."

But even in non-Marxist circles, in decrying wealth we discover that property ownership often comes up for rebuke. In the recent Occupy Wall Street Movement we saw a clear disregard of property and property rights. Charles Kadlec rightly observes:

> "Disregard, if not the abolition of property rights, is at the heart of the OWS movement. The attack on property rights begins with the act 'to occupy,' that is to take possession of someone else's property through the power of the mob. And, it is manifest in the communal nature of OWS movement."[13]

Less extreme than Marxism, socialist tendencies tend also to oppose private property rights. In an older article explaining socialism and its relationship to private property we read:

> "While perhaps no two contemporary writers who advocate socialism or some other species of collectivism have precisely the same conception of the status of property in the better order which they believe is approaching, the majority of them would probably agree that all, or most, forms of property employed in production are to be owned and

---

[12] Thomas Sowell, *The Thomas Sowell Reader* (New Yok: Basic 2011), 144

[13] Charles Kadlec, "Social Justice, Greed And The Occupy Wall Street Movement," *Forbes* (Nov. 21, 2011). http://www.forbes.com/sites/charleskadlec/2011/11/21/social-justice-greed-and-the-occupy-wall-street-movement/

operated by 'society' or 'the people' collectively and not distributively
and individually."[14]

This holds true still today.

In Scripture private property is protected, as we might surmise from
its highlighting of wealth as a blessing. In the Old Testament we find laws
that strongly secure property rights. For instance, we see landmark laws
that protect the boundaries of one's land. In Deuteronomy 27:17 we read:
"cursed is he who moves his neighbor's boundary mark" (cp. Deut. 19:14;
Prov. 22:28; 23:10). If someone damages another person's property he is
obligated to reimburse the loss (Exo. 22:4–9, 14).

The Ten Commandments are the foundational principles for all of
God's law. Two of these commandments directly defend property rights.
The sixth commandment states: "You shall not steal." Stealing requires
that property belongs to one person and not the other, as we see in the
punishment of theft: "If a man steals an ox or a sheep and slaughters it
or sells it, he shall pay five oxen for the ox and four sheep for the sheep"
(Exo. 22:1). Jesus condemns stealing by reaffirming God's law (Matt.
19:18//). The tenth commandment declares: "You shall not covet . . .
anything that belongs to your neighbor." Coveting is a necessary first
step toward theft and is itself condemned by God. Christ also condemns
covetousness (Mark 7:22).

In the New Testament we continue to see private property endorsed,
not only by a continuation of God's law in general (Matt. 5:17; 19:18//;
Rom. 2:21; 13:9), but by other means. For instance, in Acts 5 Ananias and
Sapphira sold some of their property (Acts 5:1), then claimed to be giving
all the proceeds to the apostles (Acts 5:2–3). But they lied in this and
Peter responded to their falsehood in a way that acknowledged the
property was rightly theirs: "While it remained unsold, did it not remain
your own? And after it was sold, was it not under your control?" (Acts
5:4).

The biblical worldview endorses private property rights. And in doing
so it opposes socialistic and Marxist theories of property. A biblical view
of government will affirm these property rights. Micah 2:1–2 warns
political authorities:

---

[14] William K. Wright, "Private Property and Social Justice," *International Journal
of Ethics* , 25:4 (1915): 498.

"Woe to those who scheme iniquity, / Who work out evil on their beds! / When morning comes, they do it, / For it is in the power of their hands. / They covet fields and then seize them, / And houses, and take them away. / They rob a man and his house, / A man and his inheritance."

Ezekiel 46:18 does the same: "The prince shall not take from the people's inheritance, thrusting them out of their possession; he shall give his sons inheritance from his own possession so that My people will not be scattered, anyone from his possession."

## The free market

Alongside the extolling of wealth and the securing of private property stands the concept of a free market. In a free-market economic system men can freely engage in commerce without governmental interference. Prices are not set by government but by voluntary, competitive forces in the market place.

Unfortunately, in our modern context a multiplicity of government regulations, rationing policies, price controls, minimum wage laws, and so forth negatively impact private transactions and distort the market-place. This distortion comes about by trying to deny the most basic principle of economics: scarcity. In a free market prices rise or fall in allocating resources and reflecting supply and demand. But when a government gets involved and attempts to control transactions in one way or the other, both the quantity and quality of goods diminishes. It also creates a black market that attempts to circumvent political controls.

The Bible endorses a free market where products and prices are controlled by real-world market factors rather than dream-world political influences. The previous studies on wealth and private property imply a free market, but there is more.

Interestingly, Jesus strongly endorsed a free market in his teachings. For instance, in the parable of the Laborers in the Vineyard we see free bargaining rights and the lack of price controls:

"For the kingdom of heaven is like a landowner who went out early in the morning to hire laborers for his vineyard. When he had agreed with the laborers for a denarius for the day, he sent them into his vineyard. And he went out about the third hour and saw others standing idle in the market place; and to those he said, 'You also go into the vineyard, and whatever is right I will give you.' And so they went. Again he went out about the sixth and the ninth hour, and did the same thing. And about the eleventh hour he went out and found others standing around; and he said to them, 'Why have you been standing here idle all day long?' They said to him, 'Because no one hired us.' He said to them, 'You go into the vineyard too.' When evening came, the owner of the vineyard said to his foreman, 'Call the laborers and pay them their wages, beginning with the last group to the first.' When those hired about the eleventh hour came, each one received a denarius. When those hired first came, they thought that they would receive more; but each of them also received a denarius. When they received it, they grumbled at the landowner, saying, 'These last men have worked only one hour, and you have made them equal to us who have borne the burden and the scorching heat of the day.' But he answered and said to one of them, 'Friend, I am doing you no wrong; did you not agree with me for a denarius? Take what is yours and go, but I wish to give to this last man the same as to you. Is it not lawful for me to do what I wish with what is my own? Or is your eye envious because I am generous?'" (Matt. 20:1–15)

Of course, the parable is focusing on the generosity of the landowner and therefore speaks of the grace of God as its ultimate point. But it is framed in such a way as to endorse a free market. In this parable we see the landowner looking for workers and bargaining with them regarding their pay. He pays some workers more than others. But all of them are paid the price they freely contracted.

Ultimately though, one of the workers complains about this policy. The landowner responds to this complaint: "Is it not lawful for me to do what I wish with what is my own?" This parable could be re-titled today as the Parable of the Job Creator and the Workers in that this wealthy landowner created jobs for the unemployed. And this was possible because of the free market.

## The morality of investing

All of these economic issues we have been briefly reviewing also imply the morality of investing, gaining interest, and making profits. But again, today we see many in our society decrying "obscene profits" and "exorbitant incomes." For instance, in April of 2011 "ABC's Jon Karl on Monday railed against the 'obscene' profits of the oil companies and demanded to know what House Speaker John Boehner plans to do about it."[15]

A free market, however, allows the liberty to invest and the freedom to seek good returns on an investment. The complaints against "obscene profits" overlook the benefits these profits generate: they fuel research and development of more products, offer good wages for employees throughout the oil industry, and provide ample returns for retirees invested in stocks and mutual funds.

Though God's law prohibits loaning money at interest to the needy (Exo. 22:25; Lev. 25:35–37), it encourages lending money for investments. The law specifically declares: "You may charge interest to a foreigner" (Deut. 23:20a). God's blessing on Israel increases her wealth and profitability so that she may make investments to other nations: "the LORD your God will bless you as He has promised you, and you will lend to many nations, but you will not borrow; and you will rule over many nations, but they will not rule over you" (Deut. 15:6a; cp. Deut. 28:12).

And once again we see Jesus' teaching endorsing the right of investments and profits. Though he is teaching about spiritual realities in the kingdom of God, he uses a familiar and good framework to present his lesson.

"For it is just like a man about to go on a journey, who called his own slaves and entrusted his possessions to them. To one he gave five talents, to another, two, and to another, one, each according to his own ability; and he went on his journey. Immediately the one who had received the five talents went and traded with them, and gained five more talents. In the same manner the one who had received the two talents gained two more. But he who received the one talent went away, and dug a hole in the ground and hid his master's money. Now after a long time the master of those slaves came and settled accounts with them. The one who had received the five talents came up and brought five more talents, saying, 'Master, you entrusted five talents to me. See, I have gained five more talents.' His master said to him, 'Well done, good and faithful slave. You were faithful with a few things, I will put you in charge of many things; enter into the joy of your master.' Also the one

---

[15] Scott Whitlock, "ABC Bemoans 'Obscene' Profits of Oil Company 'Behemoths,'" Tell the Truth Media Research (April 26, 2011). http://newsbusters.org/blogs/scott-whitlock/2011/04/26/abcs-jon-karl-bemoans-obscene-profits-oil-company-behemoths

who had received the two talents came up and said, 'Master, you
entrusted two talents to me. See, I have gained two more talents.' His
master said to him, 'Well done, good and faithful slave. You were faithful
with a few things, I will put you in charge of many things; enter into the
joy of your master." (Matt. 25:14–23)

Here we see a clear approval of investment returns. They even picture
the kingdom of heaven (cf. Matt. 25:1, 14). The returns might even be
called "obscene." They all came it at 100%. What is more, the parable
goes on to say:

"And the one also who had received the one talent came up and said,
'Master, I knew you to be a hard man, reaping where you did not sow
and gathering where you scattered no seed. And I was afraid, and went
away and hid your talent in the ground. See, you have what is yours.' But
his master answered and said to him, 'You wicked, lazy slave, you knew
that I reap where I did not sow and gather where I scattered no seed.
Then you ought to have put my money in the bank, and on my arrival I
would have received my money back with interest. Therefore take away
the talent from him, and give it to the one who has the ten talents.'"
(Matt. 25:24–28)

This shows a rebuke of the "lazy" slave who refused to attempt to
produce a profit.

Investments and profits are necessary for fueling economic development by encouraging research and development, producing more jobs,
providing new and better products, directing resources where they are
most needed, drawing new producers into the market, and providing
insurance in the case of an economic downturn. Politicians who pander
to an envious public by seeking to regulate or remove profits destroy
economic growth and cause economic decline.

### Conclusion

Though economics is not an interesting field for most people, it is an
important one. We are constantly faced with economic realities requiring
economic decisions and responses. Sadly today we are watching our
government go bankrupt due to unchecked spending. This is not only
indebting us today but also burdening future generations.

Politics has much to do with economics. And the Bible has much to
say about economics. The word of God presents an economic system that
extols wealth gained by righteousness. And in the process it endorses

private property, a free market, profits, and investments. The biblical approach to economics is opposed to the modern tendencies in our nation toward socialism.

Christians need to be well-informed on the biblical issues impacting economics. They need to vote in terms of their Christian worldview. They need to counter-balance the leftward trend towards socialism so popular in the world today.

## Chapter 7
# NATIONAL DEFENSE

"Blessed be the LORD, my rock, / Who trains my hands for war, / And my fingers for battle." (Psa.144:1)

## Introduction

The doctrine of sin that so motivated our forefathers in establishing our form of limited, Constitutional government, arises once again as we consider another issue of great significance for politics: war.

Because of man's war against God, he is also at war with himself as God's image. Sadly, war is necessary in a fallen world. War was not necessary in Eden, but since man's fall into sin, evil must be checked — sometimes by war. As Ecclesiastes says: "There is an appointed time for everything. And there is a time for every event under heaven . . . [including] a time to kill" (Eccl. 3:1, 3).

War is necessarily on the minds of all Americans today. Like it or not, we are at war with Islamist terrorists who have not only viciously attacked us but who are bent on destroying us by *jihad* in order to impose Islam upon the world.[1] Even in America we discover that *jihad* is accepted by many Muslims. A 2011 Pew Research Center poll noted that "21% of Muslim Americans say there is at least a fair amount of support for extremism among U.S. Muslims." Since America has about 8 million Muslims, this means that about 1,680,000 of them accept some form of *jihad*.[2]

---

[1] "Consider the issue of forced conversion in Islam, a phenomenon that has a long history with ample precedents. Indeed, from its inception, most of those who embraced Islam did so under duress, beginning with the Ridda wars and during the age of conquests, and to escape dhimmi status. This is a simple fact." Raymond Ibrahim, "Islam's History of Forced Conversions," *Middle East Forum* website. http://www.meforum.org/3056/islam-forced-conversions. See also: M. A. Khan, *Islamic Jihad: A Legacy of Forced Converson, Imperialism, and Slavery* (Bloomington, Ind.: iUniverse: 2009).

[2] "Muslim American Demographic Facts," *Allied Media Corporation* website. http://www.allied-media.com/AM/

Regarding the world situation, "recent (2009) Polls show a disparity of views regarding terrorism, with between 15% and 30% of respondents in most Muslim countries surveyed holding a positive view." It goes on to note that "an average of 30% of respondents in Indonesia, Egypt, Pakistan and Morocco held positive views of groups that launch attacks against Americans"[3] Since Indonesia itself has 220 million people, this represents around 66 million Muslims who support terrorism.

Quite naturally, then, the question of war is an important and relevant political issue.

Questions regarding military conflicts demand that we look into the legitimacy of war. As we engage political matters, we must consider the question of war from both a general moral perspective and a specifically biblical one. The question of war falls under the notion of national defense. And today national defense also involves border control and illegal immigration issues. So in this chapter I will briefly deal with the questions of military engagement and border security.

## Military Issues

Christians serve the one prophesied to come as the "Prince of Peace" (Isa. 9:6) who was to effect lasting peace (Isa. 2:4). His birth, announced by the angels of God, was seeking to establish peace: "Glory to God in the highest, and on earth peace among men with whom He is pleased" (Luke 2:14).

In keeping with prophetic pronouncement and angelic declaration, his teaching ministry confirms his peaceable intent. We serve a Savior who teaches us that "all things whatsoever ye would that men should do to you, do ye even so to them" (Matt. 7:12).[4] He commands in Matthew 5:44: "Love your enemies, bless them that curse you, do good to them that hate you, and pray for them which despitefully use you, and persecute you." He was so insistent upon this that he taught us: "whoever slaps you on your right cheek, turn to Him the other also" (Matt. 5:39).

Some Christians take the Lord's *peaceable* teachings to entail *pacifist* obligations for the Christian worldview. They believe that faithful Christians should never support war in any context. They often cite Christ's

---

[3] http://en.wikipedia.org/wiki/Muslim_attitudes_towards_terrorism

[4] We must be careful to interpret Jesus' teaching from within his God-based worldview. For instance, this directive is not to be used with rapists, sodomites, and sado-masochists.

"turn the other cheek" as "obvious" evidence in this direction. But we must note what he actually said: "whoever slaps you on your *right* check, turn to Him the other also." For someone to "slap" you on the *right* check would mean that he was giving you a *backhanded* slap (in that most people are right handed and would slap with their right hand). Christ is speaking of *individuals* seeking to settle insults and differences with a fight. This personal directive does not speak to conflicts on the national level involving security concerns.

So then, what did Jesus and the Bible that he believed and preached say about war?

### The Old Testament and war

We know that the Old Testament revelation endorsed at least certain forms of war. In Scripture Abram is commended for his war against the evil kings: "Blessed be Abram of God Most High, possessor of heaven and earth; and blessed be God Most High, who has delivered your enemies into your hand" (Gen. 14:20).

Of Israel's deliverer we read: "Moses built an altar, and named it The Lord is My Banner; and he said, 'The Lord has sworn; the Lord will have war against Amalek from generation to generation'" (Exo. 17:15–16). To Joshua the Lord said: "Do not fear or be dismayed. Take all the people of war with you and arise, go up to Ai; see, I have given into your hand the king of Ai, his people, his city, and his land."

Clearly God is not opposed to war per se. In fact, he himself is called a "warrior": "The LORD is a warrior; The LORD is His name" (Exo. 15:3). "The LORD will go forth like a warrior, / He will arouse His zeal like a man of war. / He will utter a shout, yes, / He will raise a war cry. / He will prevail against His enemies" (Isa. 42:13).

David even praised God for teaching him to fight and subduing nations under him:

> "Blessed be the LORD, my rock, / Who trains my hands for war, / And my fingers for battle; / My lovingkindness and my fortress, / My stronghold and my deliverer, / My shield and He in whom I take refuge, / Who subdues my people under me" (Psa. 144:1–2; cp. 2 Sam. 22:35; Psa. 18:34).[5]

---

[5] This psalm was left out of Roman Catholic peace activist Father Daniel Berrigan's commentary on the Psalms.

As we read these biblical verses we must remember that: "All Scripture is inspired by God and profitable for teaching, for reproof, for correction, for training in righteousness; so that the man of God may be adequate, equipped for every good work" (2 Tim. 3:16–17). At the time Paul wrote this, the New Testament was not complete; he was referring especially to the Old Testament.

### The New Testament and war

Jesus' first recorded public discourse opens with a strong confirmation of the entire Old Testament revelation:

> "Do not think that I came to abolish the Law or the Prophets; I did not come to abolish, but to fulfill. For truly I say to you, until heaven and earth pass away, not the smallest letter or stroke shall pass away from the Law, until all is accomplished. Whoever then annuls one of the least of these commandments, and so teaches others, shall be called least in the kingdom of heaven; but whoever keeps and teaches them, he shall be called great in the kingdom of heaven." (Matt. 5:17–19)

Elsewhere he rebukes those who do "not know the Scriptures" (Matt. 22:29; cp. Matt. 21:42), which for him at that time was the Old Testament. In his temptation by Satan at the beginning of his public ministry, he cites the Old Testament as his authority — citing Moses' Deuteronomy three times (Matt. 4:4; cp. Deut. 8:3; Matt. 4:7; cp. Deut. 6:16; Matt. 4:10; cp. Deut. 6:13). He was not in the least offended by the war references of the Old Testament.

Furthermore, neither John the Baptist (whom Christ highly commended, Matt. 11:7–11) nor Christ himself nor his Apostle Peter directs soldiers to quit the army. In Luke 3:14 we read of John the Baptist: "Some soldiers were questioning him, saying, 'And what about us, what shall we do?' And he said to them, 'Do not take money from anyone by force, or accuse anyone falsely, and be content with your wages.'"

In Luke 7:6–9 Jesus does the same when he commends a centurion:

> "Now Jesus started on His way with them; and when He was not far from the house, the centurion sent friends, saying to Him, "Lord, do not trouble Yourself further, for I am not worthy for You to come under my roof; for this reason I did not even consider myself worthy to come to You, but just say the word, and my servant will be healed. For I also am a man placed under authority, with soldiers under me; and I say to this

one, 'Go!' and he goes, and to another, 'Come!' and he comes, and to my slave, 'Do this!' and he does it." Now when Jesus heard this, He marveled at him, and turned and said to the crowd that was following Him, 'I say to you, not even in Israel have I found such great faith.'"

In Acts 10 Peter interacts with Cornelius, a Roman centurion. He never challenges Cornelius regarding his service in the military.

Jesus even uses war in one of his parables as an example of preparedness. "What king, when he sets out to meet another king in battle, will not first sit down and consider whether he is strong enough with ten thousand men to encounter the one coming against him with twenty thousand?" (Luke 14:31). In Revelation 19:11 Christ is pictured as one who "judges and makes war."

Hebrews 11 is the famous Hall of Faith chapter. But as a part of that parading of faithful people, it concludes with: "And what more shall I say? For time will fail me if I tell of Gideon, Barak, Samson, Jephthah, of David . . . who by faith conquered kingdoms, . . . became mighty in war, put foreign armies to flight" (Heb. 11:32, 33, 34).

In all of this we see that Scripture is not averse to war. This is because it recognizes the sinfulness of man, which sometimes makes war necessary. But Christianity also must consider the issue of:

### Christian morality and war
God's Law does not endorse all war. The Scriptures teach *principled* war, establishing moral principles for a just war (*jus ad bellum*). In fact, Deuteronomy 20 gives Israel certain laws of warfare that are to govern her conduct in the matter. The great Christian scholar Augustine (AD 354–430) stated the ironic reality of war: "War is waged in order to attain peace."[6] Because of the sinfulness of man sometimes war is the only way to peace.

In a time when our country is at war, we need to reflect upon the principles of a Just War Theory that have long been a part of the Christian worldview and western culture. In keeping with the righteous and peaceable intentions of the Christian faith, Just War Theory posits the following principles:

*1. The Principle of Just Cause*. A just war can only be fought to redress a grievous wrong suffered and must be engaged with a view to redressing

---

[6] Augustine, Letter 189 (to Boniface).

that injury. The right to self-defense is always just. We see this legally stated on the personal level in God's Law: "If the thief is caught while breaking in, and is struck so that he dies, there will be no blood guiltiness on his account" (Exo. 22:2). We see it on the social level in granting the magistrate the right to capital punishment for *prescribed* crimes: "He who strikes a man so that he dies shall surely be put to death" (Exo. 21:12). Jesus effectively endorses this principle: "whoever has no sword is to sell his coat and buy one" (Luke 22:36).

God condemns "princes [who] are like wolves tearing the prey, by shedding blood and destroying lives in order to get dishonest gain" (Eze. 22:27). The encoding of legislation in God's law regarding national armies takes the right to self defense from the personal and local levels to the national level: "Then *Amalek came and fought* against Israel at Rephidim. So Moses said to Joshua, 'Choose men for us, and go out, fight against Amalek'" (Exo. 17:8–9; cp. 1 Sam. 30:3, 18–19). The blessings of God include victory against the enemy who assails: "The Lord will cause your enemies who rise up against you to be defeated before you; they shall come out against you one way and shall flee before you seven ways" (Deut. 28:7).

*2. The Principle of Last Resort.* In matters of national relations where tensions are raised, Just War Theory seeks to insure peace and safety. Therefore, just war can only be waged as a last resort requiring that all reasonable non-violent options must be exhausted before the use of force can be justified. Even regarding cities that threatened Israel we read:

> "When you approach a city to fight against it, you shall offer it terms of peace. If it agrees to make peace with you and opens to you, then all the people who are found in it shall become your forced labor and shall serve you. However, if it does not make peace with you, but makes war against you, then you shall besiege it." (Deut. 20:10-12)[7]

*3. The Principle of Legitimate Authority.* A war is just only if it is waged by a legitimate authority. Vigilante justice and gang warfare are not God-

---

[7] Israel had God-defined borders (Gen. 15:18; Exo. 23:31; etc.) and could never legitimately possess imperialistic pretensions. This passage is not dealing with the special, limited Holy War which secured the Promised Land: "Thus you shall do to all the cities that are very far from you, which are not of the cities of these nations nearby" (Deut. 20:15).

ordained means of social conduct. In fact, these are debilitating features of social chaos evidencing the breakdown of moral order. Even just causes require just means of resolution. To plan war is to plan death, which requires duly-sanctioned moral authority. This is possessed only by the civil magistrate who is ordained to wield the sword in providing for the defense of its citizenry.

According to Paul, vengeance belongs to God who will repay the evil-doer (Rom. 12:19). Just three verses later Paul begins pointing out that God has given the right to avenge wrongdoing to the civil magistrate who is the "minister of God" in this respect (Rom. 13:1–4). "Governors [are] sent by him for the punishment of evildoers and the praise of those who do right" (1 Pet. 2:14), which includes punishment of whole nations that threaten evil against another nation.

*4. The Principle of Successful Prospect.* A war can only be just if it is fought with a reasonable chance of success. Human life is precious, in that man is created in the image of God (Gen. 1:26–27). God has a special concern for man, his highest creature: "What is man, that You take thought of him? And the son of man, that You care for him?" (Psa. 8:4; cp. Job 7:17; Psa. 144:3; Heb. 2:6–8). This, of course, prohibits suicide, even at the national level.

In a parable Jesus touches on this principle of war: "Or what king, when he sets out to meet another king in battle, will not first sit down and take counsel whether he is strong enough with ten thousand men to encounter the one coming against him with twenty thousand?" (Luke 14:31). David expresses such a concern regarding the prospect of utter defeat: "David inquired of the Lord, saying, 'Shall I pursue this band? Shall I overtake them?' And He said to him, 'Pursue, for you shall surely overtake them, and you shall surely rescue all'" (1 Sam. 30:8).

The righteous seek safety, not destruction: "My God, my rock, in whom I take refuge; my shield and the horn of my salvation, my strong-hold and my refuge; my savior, You save me from violence. . . I am saved from my enemies" (2 Sam. 22:3–4). Consequently, wide scale deaths and injury incurred in a hopeless cause are not morally justifiable, being a form of national suicide.

*5. The Principle of Peaceful Objectives.* The ultimate goal of a just war is to re-establish peace, safety, and stability. The historical goal of the kingdom of God clearly teaches this primary historical objective: "He will judge between the nations and will render decisions for many peoples; and they will hammer their swords into plowshares, and their spears into pruning hooks. Nation will not lift up sword against nation, and never again will they learn war" (Isa. 2:4). As a counter example, Islam as a religion and culture has, from its founding by Muhammad, been in a constant state of war with other cultures.

The just war goal of securing peace embodies the biblical principle that we should "not be overcome by evil, but overcome evil with good" (Rom. 12:21). David, though a "man of war" (1 Chron. 28:3), exhibits his righteous desire for peace: "Too long has my soul had its dwelling with those who hate peace. I am for peace, but when I speak, they are for war" (Psa. 120:6-7). As theologian R. J. Rushdoony observes: "Even in wartime, God's purpose, the furthering of life for the purposes of godly dominion, must be obeyed."[8]

6. *The Principle of Proportionate Means.* Just war is God-sanctioned violence. But the violence meted out in war must be proportional to the injury suffered. For instance, the laws governing capital punishment constrain the state by not allowing the magistrate to capitally punish a thief (Exo. 22:7) or to put to death the murderer's family: "Fathers shall not be put to death for their sons, nor shall sons be put to death for their fathers; everyone shall be put to death for his own sin" (Deut. 24:16).[9] Likewise, the aim of war must be constrained by principles of proportionality, according to the *lex talionis* principle of "an eye for an eye" (Exo. 21:24; Lev. 24:20f).

Rushdoony observes that "total war is prohibited, either against man or against his land."[10] Napoleon's utter humiliation of his enemies led to Prussian military instructor, Karl von Clausewitz, developing the concept of "total war." But God forbids total war:

> "When you besiege a city a long time, to make war against it in order to capture it, you shall not destroy its trees by swinging an axe against them; for you may eat from them, and you shall not cut them down. For is the tree of the field a man, that it should be besieged by you? Only the trees which you

---

[8] Rousas J. Rushdoony, *The Institutes of Biblical Law* (Vallecito, Calif.: Ross, 1973), 1:355.

[9] Those who claim court-governed capital punishment is merely revenge encoded in law must recognize severe limits on the offended: they cannot punishment the criminal immediately (without trial), torture him, punish his family, or do anything beyond the limits of the law. Capital punishment actually curtails personal revenge.

[10] Rushdoony, *Institutes*, 1:355.

know are not fruit trees you shall destroy and cut down, that you may construct siegeworks against the city that is making war with you until it falls." (Deut. 20:19–20)

*7. The Principle of Civilian Immunity.* When just war is engaged the military plans and actions must discriminate between combatants and non-combatants. Unarmed civilians are never legitimate targets of war, and every reasonable effort must be taken to avoid killing them. Civilian deaths are tolerable only as accidental, unavoidable collateral damage resulting from an attack on a legitimate military target.

The Scriptures reflect this principle in various places. Armed combatants are the target of just war: "Let not him who bends his bow bend it, / Nor let him rise up in his scale-armor; / So do not spare her young men; / Devote all her army to destruction" (Jer. 51:3).[11] Again, this embodies the principle of man being the image of God and under his protections.

### Border Issues

The borders of a country are important for its economic health, social stability, and political longevity; indeed, a nation's very existence depends on its borders. They define a country as a geographical, legal, economic, and political unit.

A national government needs clear and stable borders to mark the limits of its effective legal authority (for electing its leaders, passing its laws, establishing its courts, controlling it police, and so forth) and its direct economic control (by establishing monetary policy, levying taxes, regulating commerce, and so forth). They also are crucial for identifying those who are legally authorized to elect its leaders so that it might function politically as a free, self-governing nation.

Because of their significance, borders are like skin on the body: they are the first line of defense against intrusive, harmful influences. Consequently, borders must be recognized and protected in that they are vital to national security. Today, unfortunately, America's southern border is virtually unprotected, is a source of a massive illegal population influx, and has become a hotly-debated political topic.

---

[11] Such a limitation did not apply in the conquest of the Promised Land due to the extreme debasement of the culture that had to be removed so that a righteous culture might be established in its place.

A nation cannot exist in an amorphous state. Thus, in a book such as this we must briefly consider this matter as an important and relevant political concern, especially in that it is directly related to national security issues. Let us begin by considering the:

**Numerical problem**

Although the exact numbers of illegal immigrants in America are impossible to establish and verify, most estimates fall into a fairly close range. The Center for Immigration Studies is a leading immigration research organization in America. In an October 2011 posting, "A Record -Setting Decade of Immigration: 2000-2010," Steven A. Camarota reports:

> "New data from the Census Bureau show that the nation's immigrant population (legal and illegal), also referred to as the foreign-born, reached 40 million in 2010, the highest number in American history. Nearly 14 million new immigrants (legal and illegal) settled in the country from 2000 to 2010, making it the highest decade of immigration in American history. . . . Of this number some 10 to 12 million are likely illegal immigrants."

The problem of illegal aliens has become such a politically-charged issue in our era of political-correctness and psychologized-law that the matter is often reported under sanitized terms that confuse the issue. It is becoming more common to reject the phrase "illegal alien," even though we are speaking of aliens who are here illegally.

Rather, the more popular, politically-correct phrase is "undocumented workers," even though many of these are not workers but wives, children, and babies who do not work. Some are even criminals, gang members, and fugitives (see below). This phraseology distorts the problem by re-interpreting it. But like Lincoln once stated: Even if you call a dog's tail a leg, it still only has four legs.

Sometimes they are called "undocumented immigrants," again avoiding the term "illegal" and equating these with legal immigrants. In the first place, however, these usually are not "undocumented" immigrants for they often have fraudulent documents attained through identity theft (more about this later).

But more importantly, anyone who enters a country without a passport is deemed by law to be there *illegally* — no matter how you may prefer to think of it. In fact, on June 1, 2009, the final phase of the Western Hemisphere Travel Initiative was passed, which requires even Canadian and Mexican citizens to present a passport for entering the country. Our borders used to be open to these national neighbors virtually without restriction, but now *by law* this has been changed. Thus, anyone entering without presenting a passport is not only an alien (non-American) but *illegal* (acting against the law).

In 2010 the Pew Hispanic Center released a report on illegal immigration. According to "HuffPost Politics" Pew "said its study, based on Census data augmented by the Center's analysis, was not designed to answer why the illegal immigration population stayed steady over the past two years. Illegal immigrants made up 3.7 percent of the nation's population last year and 5.2 percent of the workforce, the report said."[12]

These are large numbers that demonstrate our border is broken. And because of the size of the numbers, our broken border is dangerous in many respects. Let us first note the problem even for the illegals regarding their own:

### Personal endangerment

Those entering the United States illegally are subject to capture, processing, and deportation by U.S. authorities. But this is the least of their worries. Those illegally crossing our southern border do so at severe physical risk from several directions.

Many illegals pay human smugglers ("coyotes") to sneak them into the country. Oftentimes these smugglers are members of ruthless Mexican drug cartels or even corrupt Mexican government officials who subject illegals to extortion, robbery, and rape. Sometimes the smugglers are human traffickers who sell the women into prostitution. Smugglers often dump illegals in the desert where they are subjected to the elements resulting in heat strokes, dehydration, and hypothermia.[13]

Others are killed in transportation accidents as the smugglers attempt to sneak them across the border in vehicles. For instance, in a

---

[12] "Illegal Immigration: Numbers Holding at 11.2 Million Despite Crackdowns," http://www.politicsdaily.com/2011/02/02/illegal-immigration-numbers-holding-at-11-2-million-despite-cra/

[13] Ray Walser, Jena Baker McNeill, and Jessica Zuckerman, "The Human Tragedy of Illegal Immigration: Greater Efforts Needed to Combat Smuggling and Violence," *The Heritage Foundation* (June 20, 2011). http://www.heritage.org/research/reports/2011/06/the-human-tragedy-of-illegal-immigration-greater-efforts-needed-to-combat-smuggling-and-violence

2006 news report we read: "the Yuma County Sheriff's Department said Tuesday that the three men and six women killed were among 21 Mexicans 'stacked like cordwood' in a Chevrolet Suburban whose driver lost control after crossing a spike strip laid down by Border Patrol agents."[14]

Others attempting to enter America by themselves endure the same consequences in the desert: strokes, dehydration, and hypothermia. Many drown trying to cross rain-swollen ditches and canals, as well as trying to swim the Rio Grande.[15] Some are killed in shoot-outs with U. S. Border Patrol. Indeed, a 2006 report by the U. S. Government Accountability Office titled "Illegal Immigration: Border-Crossing Deaths Have Doubled Since 1995" noted that: "the annual number of border-crossing deaths increased from 241 in 1999 to a total of 472 deaths recorded in 2005."[16]

All those who make it into America alive must avoid detection by U. S. authorities. Since almost all of these illegals engage in manual labor, they are easily exploited by unscrupulous employers. They are frequently underpaid and overworked in unsafe and unhealthy working conditions. Such employers also frequently breach child labor laws in those contexts.

## Social costs

Illegal immigration generates enormous social costs for our nation, both in terms of financial outlays and criminal outlaws. These costs require careful political action rather than the careless political inaction we have been witnessing. The unconcern of so many politicians has allowed the problem of illegal immigration to become a process of legal invasion.

*Identity theft.* Because of their illegal status and their desire to work in America, these aliens often engage in or are party to identity theft,

---

[14] Randal C. Archibold, "Risky Measures by Smugglers Increase Toll on Immigrants," *New York Times* (Aug. 9, 2006). http://www.nytimes.com/2006/08/09/us/09crash.html

[15] Karl Eschbach, Jacqueline Hagan, et al. (1999), "Death at the Border," *International Migration Review* 33 (1999): 2.

[16] "Illegal Immigration: Border-Crossing Deaths Have Doubled Since 1995." United States Government Accountability Office, Report to the Honorable Bill Frist, Majority Leader, U.S. Senate (August 2006), 4. See Steve King's May 5, 2006 letter at: http://www.house.gov/apps/list/hearing/ia05_king/col_20060505_bite.html

document fraud, use of stolen social security numbers, and related offenses. The Center for Immigration Studies reports that "approximately 75 percent of illegal aliens use fraudulent Social Security cards to obtain employment." In fact, the Center noted that "illegal aliens commit felonies in order to get jobs. Illegal aliens who use fraudulent documents, perjure themselves on I-9 forms, and commit identity theft in order to get jobs are committing serious offenses and are not 'law abiding.'"[17]

*Criminal activity*. We see almost daily reports in the news regarding crimes committed by — dare we say it? — "illegal" aliens. And their illegalities are not limited to "undocumented" entrance into the country and identity theft." Many of them commit violent crimes and various other felonies. Though this is a problem caused largely by federal inattention to illegal immigration, unfortunately local and state jurisdictions have to absorb the costs for investigating, arresting, prosecuting, sentencing, jailing, and supervising these criminals. Indeed, "taxpayers pay half-a-billion dollars per year incarcerating illegal alien criminals."[18]

The House Committee on Homeland Security issued an interim report:

> "summarizing its findings regarding the criminal activity and violence taking place along the Southwest border of the United States between Texas and Mexico. The Texas-Mexico border region has been experiencing an alarming rise in the level of criminal cartel activity, including drug and human smuggling.[19]

In an article titled "Take Back the Streets," Jon Feere and Jessica Vaughan provide data gleaned from Operation Community Shield of the Bureau of Immigration and Customs Enforcement (ICE). This report states that "illegal immigrants collectively represent a group that is a significant

---

[17] Robert W. Mortensen, "Illegal, but Not Undocumented: Identity Theft, Document Fraud, and Illegal Employment," *CIS* website (June 2009). http://www.cis.org/IdentityTheft

[18] Colorado Alliance for Immigration Reform. http://www.cairco.org/econ/econ.html

[19] "A Line in the Sand: Confronting the Threat at the Southwest Border," House Committee on Homeland Security, Michael T. McCaul, Chairman, 1. http://www.house.gov/sites/members/tx10_mccaul/pdf/Investigaions-Border-Report.pdf

menace to the public. 80% have committed serious crimes in addition to immigration violations, and 40% have violent crime histories."[20]

Feere and Vaughan go on to observe that "the growth of transnational gangs has been a dangerous side effect of our failure to control the U. S.-Mexico border and our tolerance for high levels of illegal immigration." They point out that "a large share of the immigrant gangsters in the most notorious gangs such as Mara Salvatrucha (MS-13), Surenos-13, and 18th Street are illegal aliens."

In 2006 a U. S. Congressman made a startling claim. In an article citing his open letter, we learn that "twelve Americans are murdered every day by illegal aliens, according to statistics released by Rep. Steve King, R-Iowa. If those numbers are correct, it translates to 4,380 Americans murdered annually by illegal aliens."[21]

*Health care.* Because of the out-of-control problem before us, "illegal aliens have cost billions of taxpayer-funded dollars for medical services. Dozens of hospitals in Texas, New Mexico Arizona, and California, have been forced to close or face bankruptcy because of federally-mandated programs requiring free emergency room services to illegal aliens."[22]

Analyzing reports from the *Los Angeles Times* and a Cato Policy Analysis release, an article in the *Journal of American Physicians and Surgeons* stated that:

> "illegal aliens' stealthy assaults on medicine now must rouse Americans to alert and alarm. . . . What is unseen is their free medical care that has degraded and closed some of America's finest emergency medical facilities, and caused hospital bankruptcies: 84 California hospitals are closing their doors. Anchor babies. born to illegal aliens instantly qualify as citizens for welfare benefits and have caused enormous rises in Medicaid costs and stipends under Supplemental Security Income and Disability Income."[23]

---

[20] Jon Feere and Jessica Vaughan, "Take Back the Streets," *CIS* website (Sept., 2008). http://www.cis.org/ImmigrantGangs

[21] Joseph Farah, "Illegal aliens murder 12 Americans daily," *WND* website (Nov. 28, 2006). http://www.wnd.com/2006/11/39031/

[22] Colorado Alliance for Immigration Reform. http://www. cairco. org/ econ /econ.html

[23] Madeleine Pelner Cosman, "Illegal Aliens and American Medicine," *Journal of American Physicians and Surgeons* 10:1 (Spring 2005), 6. http://www.jpands.org/vol10no1/cosman.pdf

This report continues:

"Illegal aliens move freely in crime sanctuary cities. In Los Angeles, San Diego, Stockton, New York, Chicago, Miami, Austin, and Houston, no hospital, physician, city employee, or police officer is permitted to report immigration violators to the Department of Homeland Security's Bureau of Immigration and Customs Enforcement (the old INS or Immigration and Naturalization Service). Los Angeles Police Department, begun in 1979 by Chief Daryl Gates, prohibits police officers from initiating police action where the objective is to discover the alien status of a person."[24]

*Taxpayer burden.* In February 2011 a meticulously-documented, eighty-eight page report titled: "The Fiscal Burden of Illegal Immigration on United States Taxpayers" stated:

- Illegal immigration costs U.S. taxpayers about $113 billion a year at the federal, state and local level. the bulk of the costs — some $84 billion — are absorbed by state and local governments.
- The financial outlay that illegal aliens cost U.S. taxpayers is an annual amount per native headed household of nearly $1,000 after accounting for estimated tax collections. The fiscal impact per household varies considerably because the greatest share of the burden falls on state and local taxpayers whose burden depends on the size of the illegal alien population in that locality.
- Education for the children of illegal aliens constitutes the single largest cost to taxpayers, at an annual price tag of nearly $52 billion. nearly all of those costs are absorbed by state and local governments.
- At the federal level, about one-third of outlays are matched by tax collections from illegal aliens. at the state and local level, an average of less than 5 percent of the public costs associated with illegal immigration is recouped through taxes collected from illegal aliens.

---

[24] Cosman, "Illegal Aliens and American Medicine," 7.

- Most illegal aliens do not pay income taxes. among those who do, much of the revenues collected are refunded to the illegal aliens when they file tax returns. many are also claiming tax credits resulting in payments from the U.S. treasury.[25]

Elsewhere in the report we read:

"to put these numbers into perspective, the net federal outlay for illegal aliens represents an annual expense of nearly $288 ($193 net) per household headed by a U.S. citizen. the average outlay at the state level for the same family is about $1,130 ($996 net), for a total of about $1,205 ($1,075 net).[26]

**Security issues**

Since our chapter especially highlights national security issues, we now come to the even more ominous reality that our porous borders are attracting Middle East terrorist interest. In this section I will simply cite a few paragraphs from a House Committee on Homeland Security report chaired by Michael T. McCaul. It provides enough information from a high-level government entity to drive home this frightful issue. Page numbers refer to the pages in the report titled: "A Line in the Sand: Confronting the Threat at the Southwest Border."[27]

On pages 2 and 3 we learn that many attempting to enter the country illegally were from countries known to harbor terrorists:

"During 2005, Border Patrol apprehended approximately 1.2 million illegal aliens; of those 165,000 were from countries other than Mexico. Of the non-Mexican aliens, approximately 650 were from special interest countries. Special interest countries are those 'designated by the intelligence community as countries that could export individuals that could bring harm to our country in the way of terrorism."

---

[25] Jack Martin and Erich A. Ruark, "The Fiscal Burden of Illegal Immigration on United States Taxpayers," 1. Published on the *FAIR: Federation for Immigration Reform* website. http://www.fairus.org/site/DocServer/USCostStudy2010.pdf? doc ID=4921

[26] Martin and Ruark, "The Fiscal Burden," 79.

[27] "A Line in the Sand: Confronting the Threat at the Southwest Border," House Committee on Homeland Security, Michael T. McCaul, Chairman. http://www.house.gov/sites/members/tx10_mccaul/pdf/Investigaions-Border-Report.pdf

Pages 4 and 5 note further that:

"In addition to the criminal activities and violence of the cartels on our Southwest border, there is an ever-present threat of terrorist infiltration over the Southwest border. Data indicates that there are hundreds of illegal aliens apprehended entering the United States each year who are from countries known to support and sponsor terrorism.

- U.S. Immigration and Customs Enforcement investigations have revealed that aliens were smuggled from the Middle East to staging areas in Central and South America, before being smuggled illegally into the United States.
- Members of Hezbollah have already entered the United States across the Southwest border.
- U.S. military and intelligence officials believe that Venezuela is emerging as a potential hub of terrorism in the Western Hemisphere. The Venezuelan government is issuing identity documents that could subsequently be used to obtain a U.S. visa and enter the country."

Providing more specific data the report adds on page 29 that:

"The data indicates that each year hundreds of illegal aliens from countries known to harbor terrorists or promote terrorism are routinely encountered and apprehended attempting to enter the U.S. illegally between Ports of Entry. Just recently, U.S. intelligence officials report that seven Iraqis were found in Brownsville, Texas in June 2006.103 In August 2006, an Afghani man was found swimming across the Rio Grande River in Hidalgo, Texas.... Items have been found by law enforcement officials along the banks of the Rio Grande River and inland that indicate possible ties to a terrorist organization or member of military units of Mexico.106 A jacket with patches from countries where al Qa'ida is known to operate was found in Jim Hogg County, Texas by the Border Patrol. The patches on the jacket show an Arabic military badge with one depicting an airplane flying over a building and heading towards a tower, and another showing an image of a lion's head with wings and a parachute emanating from the animal. The bottom of one patch read 'martyr,' 'way to eternal life' or 'way to immortality.'"

On page 32 of this report Commander of U.S. Southern Command, General James Hill, warns that:

*Political Issues Made Easy*

"the United States faces a growing risk from both Middle Eastern terrorists relocating to Latin America and terror groups originating in the region. General Hill said groups such as Hezbollah had established bases in Latin America. These groups are taking advantage of smuggling hotspots, such as the tri-border area of Brazil, Argentina and Paraguay, and Venezuela's Margarita Island, to channel funds to terrorist groups around the world."

Clearly, our porous borders and slack legal response to illegal immigration poses a serious security risk. As a result, this issue must be taken firmly hand by politicians before it is too late.

But some Christians believe that the Bible encourages a more "loving response" to illegal immigrants because of the dire circumstances leading them to leave their countries of origin. They even will point to God's law in the Old Testament as evidence we should not close the door on them. And since we are building our political case from within a Christian worldview rooted in Scripture, we must now consider the:

### Biblical principles

To understand immigration, and especially *illegal* immigration, from a biblical perspective, we should consider the following principles.

*God establishes governments to rule particular territories.* According to Scripture, God establishes civil government, which is defined by laws established to preserve order in its realm by insuring justice, protecting its citizens, and punishing evildoers.

> "He removes kings and establishes kings." (Dan. 2:21b)

> "There is no authority except from God, and those which exist are established by God. . . . For rulers are not a cause of fear for good behavior, but for evil. . . . It does not bear the sword for nothing; for it is a minister of God, an avenger who brings wrath on the one who practices evil." (Rom. 13:1b, 4)

Thus, Scripture speaks of kings ruling in particular regions (1 Sam. 14:20; 2 Sam. 5:12; 1 Chron. 14:2; 18:3; 9:8). For instance, we read of the "king of Egypt" (Gen. 40:1, 5; 41:46), "Sihon, king of the Amorites, / And Og, king of Bashan" (Psa. 135:11), "the king of Assyria" (Isa. 7:17, 20; 8:7; 10:12), and so forth.

The civil authority must protect a specific body-politic in a particular, defined land. "The king gives stability to the land by justice" (Prov. 29:4a).

Kings are to be "guardians" — of a particular land (Isa. 49:23). Those citizens under the protection of a civil authority must live in the authority's jurisdiction, that is, within its defined borders.

*God requires those in a nation to submit to its government's authority.* God has ordained the threat of punishment against those who do not obey the civil authority in the realm in which they live.

> "Every person is to be in subjection to the governing authorities . . . Whoever resists authority has opposed the ordinance of God; and they who have opposed will receive condemnation upon themselves." (Rom. 13:1a, 2)

> "Remind them to be subject to rulers, to authorities, to be obedient." (Tit. 3:1)

> "Submit yourselves for the Lord's sake to every human institution, whether to a king as the one in authority, or to governors as sent by him for the punishment of evildoers and the praise of those who do right." (1 Pet. 2:13–14)

So then, under the rule of law, a stable, just society is nurtured in a particular region. But by the very nature of the case that we are considering, illegal immigration in America is a breach of national law. The very presence of persons who have intentionally sneaked into the country without proper admission, immediately sets them against the law of the land and against a key purpose of a government's existence.

In America the Constitution requires that Congress "establish a uniform Rule of Naturalization," and it grants Congress power "to make all Laws which shall be necessary and proper for carrying into Execution the foregoing Powers, and all other Powers vested by this Constitution in the Government of the United States, or in any Department or Officer thereof" (Art. 1. sect 8).

Under this Constitutional power the federal government has passed laws for properly and legally entering the nation even for temporary visits. Section 1325 in Title 8 of the United States Code defines "Improper Entry of an Alien":

> "(a) Improper time or place; avoidance of examination or inspection; misrepresentation and concealment of facts:
>> 1. enters or attempts to enter the United States at any time or place other than as designated by immigration agents, or

2. eludes examination or inspection by immigration agents, or
3. attempts to enter or obtains entry to the United States by a willfully false or misleading representation or the willful concealment of a material fact."

These laws established by our government are intentionally being broken by illegal aliens, which is why they are designated "illegal" aliens.

*God requires that rulers keep and enforce the laws of their nation.* God holds civil rulers accountable for their conduct in office. The Deuteronomy 17 "law of the king" warns that civil rulers are not above the law, but are themselves ultimately subject to the law of the land. Therefore, the civil ruler of a realm must be careful to observe the law, just as was Israel's king: he must keep "all the words of this law and these statutes, that his heart may not be lifted up above his countrymen and that he may not turn aside from the commandment, to the right or the left" (Deut. 17:19–20a). Nehemiah confesses the sins of Israel's king in this regard: "For our kings, our leaders, our priests and our fathers have not kept Your law" (Neh. 9:34a).

Rulers are obligated to keep the covenant to which they swore. Political leaders are obliged, therefore, to uphold the laws of the land, including laws defining the nation by border control, immigration policy, and naturalization processes. If these legally-established laws need changing, they must be changed through proper process, not simply disregarded while the problem they are designed to prevent is overlooked. In our situation here in America, the president takes the following oath: "I do solemnly swear (or affirm) that I will faithfully execute the Office of President of the United States, and will to the best of my Ability, preserve, protect and defend the Constitution of the United States" (Art. 2, sect. 1).

*The Bible endorses national borders.* The Bible endorses national sovereignty and border definition. Before Israel received her land, she journeyed "until they came to the border of the land of Canaan" (Exo. 16:35). She was told that she would inherit "Canaan according to its borders" (Num. 34:2). The next few verses carefully define that border:

"The border shall turn direction from Azmon to the brook of Egypt, and its termination shall be at the sea. As for the western border, you shall have the Great Sea, that is, its coastline; this shall be your west border. And this shall be your north border: you shall draw your border line from the Great Sea to Mount Hor. You shall draw a line from Mount Hor to the

Lebo-hamath, and the termination of the border shall be at Zedad; and the border shall proceed to Ziphron, and its termination shall be at Hazar-enan. This shall be your north border. For your eastern border you shall also draw a line from Hazar-enan to Shepham, and the border shall go down from Shepham to Riblah on the east side of Ain; and the border shall go down and reach to the slope on the east side of the Sea of Chinnereth. And the border shall go down to the Jordan and its termination shall be at the Salt Sea. This shall be your land according to its borders all around." (Num. 34:5–12)

Within the Promised Land God carefully defined a portion of the land given to the Jewish tribes of Reuben and Gad: "To the Reubenites and to the Gadites I gave from Gilead even as far as the valley of Arnon, the middle of the valley as a border and as far as the river Jabbok, the border of the sons of Ammon; the Arabah also, with the Jordan as a border, from Chinnereth even as far as the sea of the Arabah, the Salt Sea, at the foot of the slopes of Pisgah on the east." (Deut. 3:16–17) The book of Joshua repeatedly defines the tribal borders (Josh. 13:26–27; 15:1–1; 16:2–8; 17:8–18; 18:12–20; 19:11–34; 22:25).

Moses taught Israel that once she entered the Promised Land (Exo. 13:5), she would celebrate the Passover, and in that celebration she was to make sure that nothing leavened "be seen among you in *all your borders*" (Exo. 13:7). Once the Philistines were subdued, "they did not come anymore within the border of Israel" (1 Sam. 7:13). The Bible mentions the borders of Edom (Num. 20:23; Josh. 15:21), Ammon (Num. 21:13; 22:36; Josh. 12:2), Moab (Num. 21:13, 15; 33:44; Deut. 2:18), and many others.

In the Old Testament national borders were respected. As Moses led Israel from Egypt to the Promised Land, he requested permission to pass through Edom (Num. 20:14–21), the Amorite territory (Num. 21:21ff), and Heshbon (Deut. 2:27). In Judges 11:17 we read the report of Israel requesting that the king of Edom let them pass through his land. When he refused they went around his (border-defined) land (Jdgs. 11:18). The same is true later under Nehemiah (Neh. 2:7).

God promises a future day in Egypt when a pillar of the Lord will be built "near its border" (Isa. 19:19). He promises that "violence will not be heard again in *your land*, / Nor devastation or destruction within *your borders*" (Isa. 60:18a). God's glory in that day, however, will be "magnified beyond the border of Israel" (Mal. 1:5b).

Citizens of border-defined nations pay taxes, submit to laws, are granted certain rights and privileges, are protected by its rulers, and so forth. The very nature of taxation requires defined borders. Taxes are not paid to a particular nation by all people in the world, but only those under the authority of a particular government (Rom. 13:7). Thus, nations must have defined borders and an established citizenry to set it off from other nations and peoples.

Furthermore, we see national borders demanded by good and necessary consequence. For instance, in Deuteronomy 4:5–8 Israel's laws were to serve as a model for the nations. Obviously those other nations did not have Israel's laws governing them, for they had their own laws that they should evaluate in the light of Israel's: "So keep and do them, for that is your wisdom and your understanding in the sight of the peoples who will hear all these statutes and say, 'Surely this great nation is a wise and understanding people'" (Deut. 4:6).

In Deuteronomy 28:49 God warns Israel that he will curse her if she rebels against him. He will curse her by bringing a foreign nation into her land to conquer and dominate her. He explains that this enemy "shall besiege you in all *your* towns until *your* high and fortified walls in which you trusted come down throughout *your land*, and it shall besiege you in all your towns *throughout your land* which the LORD your God has given you" (Deut. 28:52). But if Israel is obedient, God promises: "I shall also grant peace in the land, so that you may lie down with no one making you tremble. I shall also eliminate harmful beasts from the land, and no sword will pass through your land" (Lev. 26:6).

Just as under God's law individuals held the rights to private property (Exo. 20:15, 17; 22:8, 11; Deut. 5:21) and property landmarks (Deut. 19:14; 27:17; Prov. 22:28; 23:10–11), so nations are to have borders defining themselves. Thus, we read in Deuteronomy 32:8: "When the Most High gave the nations their inheritance, / When He separated the sons of man, / He set the boundaries of the peoples / According to the number of the sons of Israel."

And just as individual families have the right to control who enters their houses (Gen. 19:6, 10; Exo. 22:2; 24:10–11; Matt. 24:43; Luke 11:7), so does a national government have authority to control who enters its country. Similarly, cities have the right to bar people from entering (Neh. 7:3; 13:19–21).

*The Bible mentions national registries for defining a nation's citizenry.* Israel had registries of her own citizens (Num. 1:18; Eze. 13:9; cf. Psa.

87:4). These are reflected in the various recorded genealogies mentioned in Scripture (e.g., 1 Chron. 1–14). Citizens from other realms were recognized, such as "the citizens of Jericho" (Josh. 24:11), "the citizens of that country" (Luke 15:15), and the "citizens" of a "distant country" (Luke 19:12, 14). Roman citizenship could even be bought (Acts 22:28).

The nation of Israel had the right to cut off people from its membership (Exo. 12:15, 19; 30:33, 38; Lev. 7:20ff; Num. 9:13; 15:30). Certainly if she could this, she had the right to control the flow of non-citizens into the land.

*The Bible recognized aliens in the land.* Biblical law requires equal justice for all, including "strangers" and "aliens."[28] Unfortunately, these laws are often wrongly used to argue for open borders. For instance, a favorite law used in this way is Leviticus 19:33–34:

> "When a stranger resides with you in your land, you shall not do him wrong. The stranger who resides with you shall be to you as the native among you, and you shall love him as yourself, for you were aliens in the land of Egypt; I am the Lord your God." (cp. Exo. 12:49; 22:21; 23:9; Lev. 19:33; Num. 15:29; Deut. 26:12)

This law established legal protections for strangers and aliens in the nation, but it did not entail free and unlimited entry into the nation by them. In fact, it actually required Israel's defined borders and recognized citizenry — otherwise the stranger or alien would not be known to be such. Since God's law established legal distinctions between the Israelites and the aliens and strangers, by the very nature of the case, they must be known and identified if they are to be treated according to the law. All this type of law does is require that (recognized) strangers who are (legally) within Israel be treated *justly*; it says nothing about how they may enter the nation.

In fact, aliens were not obliged to keep certain of Israel's ceremonial laws; this allowed them to do certain things the Jews could not. "You

---

[28] A technical discussion of the different terms used by Scripture for non-Israelites in Israel would be cumbersome, distracting, and not entirely helpful. I would just note that different types of "aliens" and "strangers" lived in Israel. Some were traders visiting for a time to do business. Others were temporary residents who purchased property to live within the country for a longer period. Others came to Israel to become a part of the people and culture. But all were from outside of Israel's lineage and therefore subject to some distinct laws.

shall not eat anything which dies of itself. You may give it to the alien who is in your town, so that he may eat it, or you may sell it to a foreigner" (Deut. 14:21). The foreigner must be known if he were allowed to eat this food. He also must be known because he was not allowed to partake of the Passover: "The LORD said to Moses and Aaron, 'This is the ordinance of the Passover: no foreigner is to eat of it'" (Exo. 12:43).

God also allowed for Israel to require payments of debt from a foreigner in the Sabbath Year, though this was not allowed for a fellow Jew: "From a foreigner you may exact it, but your hand shall release whatever of yours is with your brother" (Deut. 15:3). Foreigners could also be charged interest on loans: "You may charge interest to a foreigner, but to your countrymen you shall not charge interest, so that the LORD your God may bless you in all that you undertake in the land which you are about to enter to possess" (Deut. 23:20). Clearly, strangers, aliens, foreigners must be known in order to come under these laws.

This distinguishing and recognizing foreigners / aliens is necessary for defensive purposes: spies must be distinguished from Israel's own citizens. Obviously, unless they are traitors, spies are people who are illegally in a land. Israel even used spies who clandestinely slipped into Canaan: Moses sent spies secretly into the land (Num. 13:2, 16–21). When Joshua was ready to enter the Promised Land to conquer it, he sent spies in "secretly" (Josh. 2:1). The sons of Dan sent spies to spy out Laish (Jdg. 18:2, 17).

*Biblical law obligates strangers and aliens.* In biblical law the "stranger" is a person residing among the Jews but separate from them. As non-citizens they were obligated to comply with Israel's law (e.g., Exo. 23:12; Lev. 16:29; 18:26; 17:13; Deut. 16:9–15). In fact, special laws governed their presence in Israel (Deut. 23:3; 24:14–15, 17–21; 26:10–13). They were even treated differently in some respects (Deut. 14:21; 15:3) — again, recognizing them as distinct from citizens.

For fully integrating into Israel, the stranger must apply for acceptance and take certain formal steps. For instance,

> "if a stranger sojourns with you, and celebrates the Passover to the Lord, let all his males be circumcised, and then let him come near to celebrate it; and he shall be like a native of the land. But no uncircumcised person may eat of it. The same law shall apply to the native as to the stranger who sojourns among you" (Exo. 12:48–49).

They were not automatically included in the full life and privileges of the nation.

Thus, in all of this we see that the justice due an alien is the justice called for by obedience to the law (Deut. 24:17; 27:19). But law obedience contradicts any idea of their illegal presence in the land.

### Final thoughts

As Thomas Sowell has observed:"The purpose of immigration laws and policies is to serve the national interest of this country. There is no inherent right to come live in the United States, in disregard of whether the American people want you here."[29]

Unfortunately, some politicians and civil rights advocates are promoting across-the-board amnesty for illegal aliens currently in America. To grant such would be intolerable. It would publicly endorse the breaking of properly-enacted laws, create a lure for further chain migration by millions of relatives of the illegal aliens received en masse, and send a signal to millions of people throughout the world to attempt illegal entry. In the process it would deluge America's immigration system, deplete financial resources, distort the labor market, defer the costs to law-abiding citizens, detract from personal and national security, and discourage those seeking a proper immigration status.

### Conclusion

In this chapter we have considered two issues related to national security: the legitimacy of military power for communal defense, and the importance of securing our own borders from illegal immigration.

The right for a nation to wage war has long been maintained in Christian culture — because it was necessitated by sin in the world and established in biblical law as a means of protecting a nation. God's word and the Christian worldview arising from it must guide us in this most fearsome power of government. God's word directs us in all of life, and is especially important in governing that which can end life and destroy society.

The right for a nation to define and secure its own borders is also important in the political debate. By divine design, government has been

---

[29] Thomas Sowell, "Gingrich and Immigration," *National Review* (Nov. 29, 2011). http://www.nationalreview.com/articles/284245/gingrich-and-immigration-thomas-sowell

established to protect its citizens; by Constitutional right our government must "insure domestic Tranquility, provide for the common defence, [and] promote the general Welfare, and secure the Blessings of Liberty to ourselves and our Posterity" (Preamble to the Constitution). How can it do so if our Constitutional authorities will not protect our borders?

Why should American citizens obey the law if we see our own federal government not seeking to enforce it? Allowing illegal immigration discourages citizens as well as sets a bad example for them. Tolerating illegal activities undermines the rule of law.

As someone has noted on this matter: "If you want to understand the dangers of unchecked immigration, just talk to an American Indian." America is a nation built by immigrants who are welcomed through legal channels; but it is also a nation established on law.

# Chapter 8
# PATIENT PROGRESS

"The kingdom of God is like a man who casts seed upon the soil; and he goes to bed at night and gets up by day, and the seed sprouts and grows." (Mark 4:26–27)

## Introduction

In this book I have presented several important issues regarding politics. I opened with three general matters necessary for guiding Christian thinking in this field (chs. 1–3). Then I highlighted a few specific matters of national concern (chs. 6–7).

First, I noted that the Christian worldview necessarily encompasses politics, and therefore expects Christians to bring their Bible-based convictions to bear on it. Second, I pointed out that Christians did in fact influence the founding of America and the framing of her government, thereby presenting historical evidence of Christian convictions actually impacting political issues. Third, I noted that politics is an intrinsically moral concern that requires a transcendent, religious source that only Christianity can offer. This demands that we seek to influence our political culture.

After laying down these foundation stones, I applied biblical principles to a few select issues facing our nation today. In chapter 4 I highlighted some of the implications of our foundational law in the Constitution. In chapter 5 I focused on an important implication of our Constitution: limited powers for government. Chapter 6 emphasized the free-market nature of our economic system, which is founded in Scripture and established in American constitutional law. Finally in chapter 7 I noted the importance of national defense and border control for maintaining our constitutional government.

Now before closing, I would like to reflect on our political hopes and strategies for a strong Christian influence on America's future. But before I get into this question, we must recognize our nation's political structure.

America is a republic, not a democracy. Rather than being a democracy run directly by the people, we are a republic in which we elect our officials and empower them to make decisions on our behalf. The word "democracy" never appears in our Constitution, whereas it specifically states that "the United States shall guarantee to every State in this Union a Republican Form of Government" (Art. 4; § 5). We are reminded of this important reality whenever we repeat our Pledge of Allegiance, for we the pledge is "to the *republic* for which it stands." The fundamental purpose of our Constitution is to direct our national government in how to operate as a republic.

Nevertheless, in our constitutional republic we elect our government officials by majority vote. The Constitution states that members of the House of Representative are to be elected "by the People of the several States" (Art. 1; § 2). Originally Senators were elected by state legislators (who themselves were elected by the people): "The Senate of the United States shall be composed of two Senators from each State, chosen by the Legislature thereof" (Art. 1 Sect. 3). The Seventeenth Amendment (ratified, April 8, 1913), however, changed this, insuring "two Senators from each State, elected by the people thereof." The President is elected indirectly by the people through the choosing of Electors by the (popularly elected) legislatures of each state (Art. 2; § 1). This system insures that each state, regardless of size, will be proportionally represented in the presidential election.

Thus, every adult citizen of the United States (unless he is a felon) has the right to vote. And as Christians our worldview obligates us to vote so that we might exercise a righteous influence on the governance of the nation. But now the rub. Though Christians are well-represented in America, two problems reduce our influence: (1) we do not represent a majority of the population, and (2) we are not in agreement among ourselves regarding political matters.

As a consequence of our present circumstances, we have few really good candidates from which to choose for our leaders. What are we to do? How shall we operate in such a mixed political environment? I would like to offer direction for what we as Christian citizens should do. As I begin I will first consider:

### Our Current Dilemma

Because there are so few candidates operating on strongly-held biblical principles, and because more often than not those few good ones have little chance of winning a general election, we find ourselves facing a dilemma. The voting quandary we face is known as "the lesser of evils." That is, if we as voters are in a political election involving several candidates and we realize that the best candidate cannot win, what are we to do? We face the prospect of either voting for our preferred candidate, knowing that he will lose, or voting for an alternative, more viable but less acceptable candidate with the hope that he will defeat the other even lesser qualified candidate. In this case the alternative candidate becomes the "lesser of evils" remaining among those who have a good chance of being elected.

Politically-conservative voters — and especially, *Christian* conservative voters — have a particularly difficult time facing this prospect. We are committed to principles rather than pragmatics. Consequently, voting for someone who is politically deficient in several respects is a hard pill to swallow, especially when there is a strongly-Christian candidate in the race. After all, we hold the truths of Scripture without compromise and are commanded in Scripture to "stand firm in the faith" (1 Cor. 16:13; cp. 2 Cor. 1:24; Gal. 5:1; Eph. 6:1, 13, 14; Phil. 1:27; 4:1; 1 Thess. 3:8; 2 Thess. 2:15; 1 Pet. 5:12). Indeed, our eternal destinies depend on such! How can we compromise our convictions in a political election? How can we vote for the lesser of two evils?

Many devout Christians, therefore, even urge us not to consider voting for the lesser of evils. For instance, a website called "Defending. Contending" states: "my current position is that true Christians should not have to vote if they first have to sit down and estimate which candidate is the lesser of two evils."[1] Peter Diezel puts it more forcefully: "I just can't get myself to believe that it is good to vote for evil. The last I heard, the lesser of two evils is still evil."[2]

Dean Isaacson of the strongly-Christian Constitution Party concurs. He complains that:

> "a vote for the lesser of two evils is still a vote for evil. If you are willing to compromise your principle for the sake of winning, don't be surprised when the candidate you voted for compromises his. Isaiah warns us that if we do not stand firm in our faith, we will not stand at all (Isa. 7:9). Paul tells us, in Ephesians chapter six, after we have done everything to stand,

---

[1] "Pilgrim" on the "Defending Contending" website (June 6, 2009). http://defendingcontending.com/2011/06/09/should-christians-vote-for-the-lesser-of-two-evils/

[2] Peter Diezel, "Voting for the Lesser of Two Evils Is Evil." "Word of His Grace" website (May 9, 2008). http://www.wordofhisgrace.org/evilisevil.htm

we must stand and stand firm. Therefore, principle-attending to the laws of God must be our absolute goal. Our convictions dictate that we cannot win using the same strategies as the moderates, liberals and neo-conservatives. We do not win by building big tents and coalitions. In fact, we are not commanded to win; Christ taught us to be faithful."[3]

These are strong words representing vigorous evangelical challenges to Christians considering voting for a candidate lacking the full panoply of conservative convictions. And as I have been urging throughout this book, we certainly must bring our firmly-held Christian worldview to bear upon the political order. What are we to think of these challenges? How are we to respond to the challenge of the lesser of evils?

I believe that though these comments are well-intended, and though they have a surface plausibility, they ultimately fail as a proper Christian response to our predicament. Let me explain from a conservative-political and a Bible-based Christian perspective why I would say this, by noting:

## Our Christian Response

In allowing the lesser-of-evils approach to voting from a Christian perspective, I would have us first note the principles involved, then consider their theological and biblical justifications. I present the question of principles first to introduce the argument; then I will show why I believe we can endorse it from within a Christian worldview.

### The Question of Principle

We need carefully to reflect on the question of principle itself, which I will do under several headings.

*First, distinguishing our principles.* When we are engaging in politics we must be careful not to place our political actions (e.g., voting) on the same level as our doctrinal commitments (i.e., faith in Scripture). We must be careful not to develop a messianic political outlook. That is, we should not believe that if we can only elect the right candidate he will save our nation. Unfortunately, as Christians we can be so earnest in our desire for a better America that we can slide into this messianic conception of politics. This allows us to become so enamored with a

---

[3] Dean Isaacson, "Pragmatism Is Not Compatible with Biblical Principle," (2000). http://www.constitutionpartyofwa.com/forms/Brochure-Responsible ChristianVoting.pdf

particular candidate as the "right" one, that we see him as our great hope who will bring forth justice, peace and prosperity.

This problem of viewing political principles as if they are on the same level as doctrinal convictions is quite widespread. For instance, consider the "Defending Contending" website cited above. Notice how the writer ("Pilgrim") sets up the debate: "true Christians should not have to vote if they first have to sit down and estimate which candidate is the lesser of two evils." This writer is classifying "true" Christians by their voting rather than by their doctrinal commitments and personal lifestyle. This type of thinking apparently believes that "by their votes you shall know them."

Our doctrinal convictions differ from our political actions in that they are immune from revision. Doctrinal convictions are rooted in the complete and permanent revelation of God in Scripture. Of course, our political *positions* should be rooted in our *understanding* of Scripture so that they are relatively secure commitments. But our political *actions* are not drawn directly from the Bible, and they are caught up in a system built on the necessity of compromise. We do not vote for our doctrinal convictions. Political actions are not on the same level as doctrinal convictions. They also invariably involve a commitment to fallen men and their political promises.

Evangelical Christian theologian J. I. Packer has wisely observed:

> "Political compromise, the basic maneuver [of politics], is quite a different thing from the sacrificing of principles. Whatever may be true in the field of ethics, compromise in politics means not the abandonment of principle, but realistic readiness to settle for what one thinks to be less than ideal when it is all that one can get at the moment. The principle that compromise expresses is that half a loaf is better than no bread."[4]

*Second, establishing our principles.* Those Christians who argue that we must vote for the "right" candidate because of our principles overlook an important issue: the problem of competing principles. What do I mean?

Let us take as one example a commitment to "constitutional government." Usually conservative Christians desire a candidate who will oper-

---

[4] J. I. Packer, "How to Recognize a Christian Citizen," Christianity Today Institute in *Christianity Today*, 29: 7 (April 19, 1985), 7.

ate on constitutional principle. Now suppose three candidates are running for a particular office. Candidate A is promoting a platform based on strong constitutional commitments. Candidate B has some strong positions but is weak in other areas. Candidate C has little interest in maintaining constitutional policies and is promoting a platform clearly antithetical to the Constitution. But now suppose (as is often the case) that Candidate A has dismal poll numbers that indicate a virtually certain landslide loss.

The strongly-committed Constitutionalist Christian now faces a dilemma. He loves Candidate A's platform, but recognizes that he almost certainly will go down to defeat. He knows that if he votes for Candidate A, then he is ultimately helping Candidate C by drawing off pro-Constitutional voters. Consequently, he decides to vote for semi-Constitutional Candidate B over anti-Constitutional Candidate C. By this action he is acting in a lesser-of-evils manner. But is he thereby acting in an unprincipled manner? No! Indeed, it is quite the opposite. Let me explain.

Since the Christian voting for the lesser of evils has strongly-held pro-Constitution principles, his basic political commitment is to defend and promote constitutional government. Therefore, in light of the very real circumstances he is facing, he is acting on virtually the *same principle* as the Christian who would only vote for Candidate A. That is, he is voting to support the Constitution by recognizing that if Candidate C were elected he would radically undermine it. He is voting therefore to *limit* the damage done to our Constitutional form of government. Therefore, by voting for Candidate B his principles regarding Constitutional government have led him to defend the Constitution *as best he can* in the *current circumstances* by opposing the greater, more dangerous enemy of the Constitution. Had he voted for Candidate A (who was certain to lose), then Candidate C would effectively be gaining a vote which would allow him to gain more anti-Constitutional influence in the long run.

By voting for the lesser of evils, the Christian is operating in terms of *principled realism*. The other Christian who will only vote for the "pure" candidate is voting in terms of *idealism*. The principled realist engages in a stop-loss voting with a long-term hope for the day when more greatly committed Constitutionalists will be able to win an election. Voting for a sure loss is like saying: "Be warmed and filled." Your heart (i.e., principle) is right but your actions (i.e., voting) are unhelpful (even harmful).

Let me provide a helpful illustration of how principled realism (lesser of evils voting) can lead to a better outcome than idealism, while attempting to hold the line. Consider a parallel situation to the electoral process just stated. This one involves a deeply-held principle but has real-world results that are more quantifiable: abortion. Evangelical pro-life Christians deem abortion as an evil that clearly undermines the very sanctity of human life.

But now let us consider a scenario presenting itself to a Christian Congressman. Say two bills are presented in the House of Representatives regarding abortion. Both of these bills are being offered in our current legal climate which allows abortion-on-demand (abortion for any and all reasons) throughout the nation. Bill A takes a strong pro-life position by making all abortions illegal. Bill B takes a largely pro-life position by declaring most abortions illegal except in the case of the potential death of the mother or rape or incest.

Now suppose that a straw vote has clearly shown that the strongly pro-life Bill A would go down to a resounding defeat, but that the largely pro-life Bill B could win the House vote. For which bill should the Christian Congressman vote? He wants to stop abortion. But if he votes for Bill A which is destined to defeat, abortion-on-demand remains the law of the land. If, however, he votes for Bill B then abortions will be largely curtailed. Tragically, if he stands on his *idealism* and refuses to vote for the lesser bill, he will have consigned tens of thousands of pre-born babies to death. On principle.

Choosing the lesser evil may be likened to an innocent person being wrongly convicted of a murder. In court he would have his lawyer seek prison time over execution. The lesser evil (prison) buys him time to seek his freedom in the future. Death, being much more permanent, removes the opportunity of future reversal of his fortunes.

Those who decry lesser-of-evils voting as mere pragmatism which rejects principle operate by faulty logic. Aaron Blumer explains this problem:

> "The truth is that there are at least three approaches to the relationship between conscience (principle) and practical results:
> 1. Pragmatism: practical results are always decisive and are all that matter.
> 2. Idealism: practical results are completely irrelevant; only principle matters.
> 3. Principled realism: practical results are part of the principle that matters."[5]

---

[5] Aaron Blumer, "Why Vote for the Lesser of Two Evils," *Sharper Iron* website (Dec. 13, 2011). http://sharperiron.org/article/why-vote-for-lesser-of-two-evils.

Thus, Blumer observes that an unstated premise is at work in the argument against principled realism. That unstated premise is that practical matters have nothing to do with conscience. But this is erroneous. Two of these approaches allow the Christian to vote his conscience (#2 and #3). Therefore, two of these approaches stand on principle, one realistically (#3) and one idealistically (#2). One of these two approaches has positive practical results (#3); the other, negative practical results (#2). By this I mean that approach #3 strives to preserve as many principles as possible against large-scale opposition, while approach #2 holds a full panoply of firmly-held principles — but effectively allows them to be washed away by employing an all-or-nothing strategy.

Surely as Christians we should strive to do what we morally can to resist evil. In fact, this should be one of the basic principles of Christian social concern. But consider our a position today: we usually have voting choices that are imperfect, but nevertheless have the opportunity to vote *against* the "greater evil." Since the very best candidate often has no chance of winning, should we not vote in a way that *effectively* opposes the greater evil? Is this not a good principle — *in light of our circumstances*? Why let the greater evil have the victory because we approach politics as an all-or-nothing proposition?

*Third, evaluating our principles.* We are considering political issues in this book, and are especially focusing on voting as an important political act that Christians should pursue. As believers we often find ourselves and our principles under assault. One of our principles should be to strive to protect our other principles as best we can against the majority opposition. I am arguing that, given our circumstances, we sometimes have to act as principled realists and vote for the lesser of evils in defending our principles for the long haul. Just as freedoms may be lost incrementally, they may also be re-established incrementally.

Unfortunately, many idealistic Christians will reject any call to voting for the lesser of evils. Sometimes they will ask: "As a Christian why would you vote for the lesser of evils?" The answer, of course is: "Because I want less evil."

Some of these will indignantly rebuke principled-realist Christians by complaining that they should *never* vote for the lesser of evils. But when considered from a Christian perspective, this position is self-refuting and borders on a messianic conception of politics. After all, Christians should be aware that unless Christ is on the ballot *every vote is for the lesser of evils*. Does not Jesus say: "No one is good except God alone" (Mark 10:18b). In fact, he can even speak to his followers as children of the "heavenly Father" and yet call them "evil": "If you then, being evil, know how to give good gifts to your children, how much more will your heavenly Father give the Holy Spirit to those who ask Him?" (Luke 11:13).

In opposing the lesser of evils the Christian could not even vote for the Apostle Paul, for he says of himself: "I am of flesh, sold into bondage to sin. . . . For the good that I want, I do not do, but I practice the very evil that I do not want. . . . I find then the principle that evil is present in me, the one who wants to do good" (Rom. 7:14, 19, 21). He even cites the Old Testament's universal declaration: "There is none righteous, not even one" (Rom. 3:10).

Because of these realities no conservative Christian can avoid voting for the lesser of evils. A vote for the Apostle Paul would be — on Paul's own admission — a lesser of evils! No candidate in this fallen world is perfect; all candidates have some flaws, some "evil." In such a world we cannot escape lesser-of-evils voting.

Taking this a step further, I would argue that an attempt to vote for a "perfect" candidate by voting third-party in *national* presidential elections is unrealistic, risky, and self-defeating. It is unrealistic because excellent third party candidates fare miserably and embarrassingly in presidential elections. They have absolutely no chance of winning. And as a consequence they project the appearance of an ineffectual, backwater Christianity with little or no clout.

This can be demonstrated statistically. In the 2000 election Patrick Buchanan of the Reform Party (deemed by many Christians as an excellent candidate) garnered only 448,895 votes out of 105,405,100 cast. This translates to 0.42 % of all votes. Howard Phillips, a strong Christian representing the biblically-faithful Constitution Party received only 98,020 votes, for 0.09% of the vote. In the 2004 election the Constitution Party candidate received only 144,499 votes, for 0.12% of all votes. In 2008 the Constitution Party garnered only 199,880 votes or 0.15% of the total.

Voting third party is also risky. The following statistics are not endorsing one candidate over the other, but are used to illustrate how just a few votes can make a difference in an election.

In the presidential election of 2000 a *very few* votes allowed George Bush to defeat Al Gore. In that remarkable election (which was so close that the winner was not determined until December 12th, over a month after the election), Bush lost the popular vote but won on the basis of the Electoral College vote. Gore, the Democratic candidate, received 50,999,897 votes to Bush's 50,456,002. That is, he won 48.38% to Bush's 47.87%. But Bush won the Electoral College vote that decided the election — *due to Florida's extremely tight voting results*. Thus, Bush won the presidency because he won Florida (with its sizeable Electoral College votes), and he won Florida by only 537 votes (a victory of 0.061%). In that Florida vote, Howard Phillips received 1,378 votes and Patrick Buchanan 17,412. Had these two candidates received just 538 more votes between them, the race would have gone the opposite way.

Tragically, Hitler won Germany on a divided vote. "Hitler became Germany's chancellor (prime minister) without ever having received more than 37 percent of the popular vote in the elections he had entered."[6] This shows the risky nature of third party candidacies. Split votes can often produce horrible results. Six million Jews paid with their lives on the basis of a split vote — as ultimately did over 40 million who died in the European theater of World War 2.

*Fourth, explaining our principles.* The principled realist recognizes the nature of our American political system: it is virtually impossible statistically for a third-party candidate to win. Generally, they only cause one of the two major party candidates to lose, such as Ross Perot in 1992. In 1992 George H. W. Bush was projected to win as much as 55% of the vote, coming off high approval ratings and a rather week unknown governor from Arkansas. But with Perot's entry into the race and his securing of 18.91% of the vote, Bill Clinton won with only 43.01% of the national vote. Clinton never was elected by a majority vote in either of his two presidential wins.

Idealists often encourage third-party candidates by arguing: "this candidate or that party provides a dream platform." That may well be true, but we have to wake up on the day after the election and realize the dream is over (or in the case of the 2000 election, we would have to sleep for a little over a month). We need to live in the real world rather than a dream world.

Some challenge the lesser-of-evils approach by arguing that it is simply a choice of fast poison (the bad candidate) versus slow poison (the

---

[6] "Hitler and Germany: 1927–35," *Macro-History and World Report* website. http://www.fsmitha.com/h2/ch16.htm

tolerable candidate). They ask: "Why prefer slow poison over fast poison?" I would ask: Which would you prefer to accidentally ingest if you were thirty minutes from a hospital? In politics, if we have to vote for "slow poison," we can at least buy some time to work on a "cure." After all, the worst candidate often wins when conservative votes are drawn away to dream candidates. By drawing votes away from a tolerable but electable candidate you are actually taking fast-acting poison by default.

Others ask: "Why do we keep voting the same way (for centrist candidate) but expect different results (Christian- principled leaders)?" This question is a two-edged sword for it can be turned on the Christian idealist: "Why do some Christians keep voting for third party candidates and watching their candidate be demolished (receiving less than 1% of the vote), while allowing their votes effectively to be siphoned off to the more liberal candidate?" Beating our head against the wall in small numbers is not a good game plan.

But now we must consider:

## The Question of Theology

As Christians living in God's world, we must understand that we are here in the world for the long run. And as we come to grips with this it will be encouraging to recognize an important method of God's dealings with man: gradualism, or incrementalism. That is, God generally works gradually over time to accomplish his purpose. We must therefore be willing to labor for our Christian influence in politics over time, not expecting all to be accomplished over night.

This theological principle should buttress our hope for the future. It allows us to seek smaller, stop-loss victories now with a goal to winning larger ones as history unfolds. Thus, this theological principle shows the practical wisdom in accepting compromise in our political actions (not compromise of our principles themselves) in the present time with a view to gaining influence in the long run. Rather than approaching politics as an all-or-nothing venture, we must recognize the significance of incremental victory over time.

In Scripture we find the principle of gradualism embodied in the actions of God in history. God works by slow providence over time by means of a "here a little; there a little" gradualism (Isa. 28:10). Indeed, he encourages his people by rhetorically asking: "who has despised the day of small things?" (Zech. 4:10).

For instance, we see divine gradualism at work in various theological issues in the Bible.

*Creation.* God created the universe on a gradualistic principle — an accelerated gradualism, to be sure, but gradual nonetheless. God created the universe step-by-step over a period of six days, though he could have easily created it all at once in an instant. "For in six days the LORD made the heavens and the earth, the sea and all that is in them" (Exo. 20:11a; cp. Gen. 1:1–31; Exo. 31:17).

*Redemption.* God promised redemption just after the entry of sin into the human race in Eden (Gen. 3:15). Yet its accomplishment follows thousands of years after Adam when Christ comes. "But when the fullness of the time came, God sent forth His Son, born of a woman, born under the Law, so that He might redeem those who were under the Law, that we might receive the adoption as sons" (Gal. 4:4–5; cp. Eph. 1:10). Our chapter-heading verse speaks to this gradualism (Mark 4:26–27).

*Revelation.* God did not give us his entire, written revelation all at once. Rather he gradually unfolded his Word to men over a period of some 1,500 years, from Moses's writings (1450 BC) until the last of the New Testament was written in the first century. "God, after He spoke long ago to the fathers in the prophets in many portions and in many ways, in these last days has spoken to us in His Son" (Heb. 1:1–2a; cp. 1 Pet. 1:10–12).

*Sanctification.* Even in God's gracious salvation he works gradually in our lives. Though our justification brings salvation as a once-for-all *act* (Rom. 4:2–3; 5:1), God works sanctification within us by an ongoing *process* throughout our lives. "Like newborn babies, long for the pure milk of the word, so that by it you may *grow* in respect to salvation" (1 Pet. 2:2; cp. Phil. 2:12-13).

It is difficult for us to be patient in a day of freeze-dried this and instant-that where scientists can measure actions in nanoseconds. But God teaches us in his Word to work patiently for the long run. We should not be dismayed if our political activities do not produce instant fruit. Sometimes we must expect less than we would hope for — by voting for the lesser evil.

But now how does this all square with:

## The Question of Scripture

In this book I am promoting a Christian worldview rooted in Scripture. But how can we encourage Christians to compromise in their voting while maintaining their worldview? The question of compromise is particularly significant for Christians who are uncompromisingly committed to Scripture. So then, does the question of compromise undermine all the practical arguments brought up by Christian idealists?

This is an important matter to consider — especially in that it frequently arises in *Christian* political discussions. Does the Bible have anything to say regarding the question of compromise? Actually it does. It allows realistic, principled compromise. Consider the following examples.

*The law of God.* God's law prohibited any labor on the Sabbath. For instance in Exodus 35:2–3 we read: "For six days work may be done, but on the seventh day you shall have a holy day, a sabbath of complete rest to the LORD; whoever does any work on it shall be put to death. You shall not kindle a fire in any of your dwellings on the sabbath day." Exodus 34:22 commands cessation of labor even during plowing and harvest times: "You shall work six days, but on the seventh day you shall rest; even during plowing time and harvest you shall rest."

Nevertheless, despite these clear prohibitions, Jesus himself taught that there are practical situations in which one may work on the Sabbath: "You hypocrites, does not each of you on the Sabbath untie his ox or his donkey from the stall and lead him away to water him?" (Luke 13:15). "Which one of you will have a son or an ox fall into a well, and will not immediately pull him out on a Sabbath day? This is not a compromise of God's Law, but is a practical *application* of God's Law in grievous circumstances.

*Jesus' practice.* Christ specifically compromised on a matter so as not to cause offense. As the Son of God he was not required to pay the two-drachma tax. Nevertheless we read in Matthew:

> "When they came to Capernaum, those who collected the two-drachma tax came to Peter and said, 'Does your teacher not pay the two-drachma tax?' He said, 'Yes.' And when he came into the house, Jesus spoke to him first, saying, 'What do you think, Simon? From whom do the kings of the earth collect customs or poll-tax, from their sons or from strangers?' When Peter said, 'From strangers,' Jesus said to him, 'Then the sons are exempt. However, so that we do not offend them, go to the sea and throw in a hook, and take the first fish that comes up; and when you open its mouth, you will find a shekel. Take that and give it to them for you and Me.'" (Matt. 17:24–27)

He could have affirmed his immunity from paying the tax, which would have underscored his claim to his deity. But here he "compromised" on that particular issue and paid the tax — so as not to cause offense.

In fact, consider the following situation. Rome was a pagan nation dominating Israel, and each legion carried an idolatrous Standard (Signums) for their identification. The Jewish historian Josephus was an eyewitness to the destruction the Jewish temple in AD 70. He reported that the Romans "carried their standards into the temple court and, setting them up opposite the eastern gate, there sacrificed to them, and with rousing acclamations hailed Titus as imperator" (*Wars* 6:6:1). The church father Tertullian (AD 160–220) writes: "The camp religion of the Romans is all through a worship of the standards, a setting the standards above all gods" (*Apology* 16).

Nevertheless, though Jesus interacted with Roman soldiers he never encouraged them to leave the army (Matt. 8:5–13).[7] Neither did John the Baptist when directly asked by soldiers "what shall we do?" (Luke 3:14).

Jesus employs an illustration in his parabolic teaching that recognizes that we must think in terms of practical solutions and be willing to compromise as we look to larger goals.[8] He taught twin parables on discipleship that employed strategic compromise for securing our ultimate goals.

"For which one of you, when he wants to build a tower, does not first sit down and calculate the cost to see if he has enough to complete it? Otherwise, when he has laid a foundation and is not able to finish, all

[7] By special privilege for Israel, Rome did not bring such images into Jerusalem.

[8] The parables themselves are actually teaching the cost of discipleship, and ultimately *not* calling for compromise. But the illustrations he uses are from the practical world regarding acceptable actions. We are focusing on the real-world illustration rather than the *spiritual-life* implication of discipleship. As one commentator notes: "Jesus constructs these parables along parallel lines: a hypothetical, demanding enterprise + analysis of the adequacy of existing resources vis-à-vis the requisite resources for achieving a successful conclusion to the enterprise + outcome when available resources fall short." Joel B. Green, *The Gospel of Matthew* (NICNT) (Grand Rapids: Eerdmans, 1997), 566.

who observe it begin to ridicule him, saying, 'This man began to build and was not able to finish.'[9]

"Or what king, when he sets out to meet another king in battle, will not first sit down and consider whether he is strong enough with ten thousand men to encounter the one coming against him with twenty thousand? Or else, while the other is still far away, he sends a delegation and asks for terms of peace." (Luke 14:28–31)

In the second parable, the king here planning for battle surely has a desire for victory. Yet as he looks realistically at his prospects he realizes the potential for loss. Consequently, he begins working on a compromise to settle the differences with the opposing king.

*Paul's practice.* In Acts 15 the Jerusalem council (which included Paul, Acts 15:12, 22) dealt with the question of circumcision. This issue was divisive and controversial in the early church because of Jewish converts to Christ (Acts 15:1, 5). The council rejected circumcision as necessary for Christians (Acts 15:1, 19, 23–29). It then sent Paul and Barnabas to Antioch, Syria, and Cilicia with the council's letter stating this.

As Paul was in the very process of delivering the letter from the Jerusalem council (Acts 16:4), he went to Derbe (Acts 16:1) and met up with Timothy. Then we read the remarkable notice that "Paul wanted this man to go with him; and he took him and circumcised him because of the Jews who were in those parts, for they all knew that his father was a Greek" (Acts 16:3)!

Of course, Paul was not compromising the *principle* by declaring that Timothy actually did need circumcision in order to be saved. But he did nevertheless circumcise Timothy — and that for a *practical* reason: so as not to offend the Jews. And he did so in the very historical context of his delivering a letter from the Jerusalem council declaring that circumcision was unnecessary. A heated context that caused "great dissension and debate" (Acts 15:2), even "much debate" (Acts 15:7).

In fact, Paul even denounced those who demanded circumcision for Christians: "Behold I, Paul, say to you that if you receive circumcision,

---

[9] The implied compromise is that the man desiring to build a tower may have to drop the building project because of the likely failure to finish the project. He obviously wanted the tower, but he saw failure looming over the project, so would surely dismiss it.

Christ will be of no benefit to you" (Gal. 5:2). This was a foundational principle for his doctrine of free grace. Yet not only did he have Timothy circumcised, during that same general time frame he wrote to the Corinthians stating that:

> "to the Jews I became as a Jew, so that I might win Jews; to those who are under the Law, as under the Law though not being myself under the Law, so that I might win those who are under the Law; to those who are without law, as without law, though not being without the law of God but under the law of Christ, so that I might win those who are without law." (1 Cor. 9:20–21)

Of course, he never changed his *conviction* (principle) that circumcision was not necessary for salvation, yet he altered his *action* for *practical* (pragmatic) goals: to persuade Jews of the gospel.

Elsewhere Paul derisively refers to circumcision as "mutilation": "Beware of the dogs, beware of the evil workers, beware of the false circumcision; for we are the true circumcision, who worship in the Spirit of God and glory in Christ Jesus and put no confidence in the flesh" (Phil. 3:3). The word translated "false circumcision" is *katatome*, which literally means "mutilation." He is using a play on words: the Jews offer *katatome* when they practice *peritome* ("circumcision").

Paul even forthrightly teaches that "true circumcision" is not of the flesh but of the heart (Rom. 2:28–29; cp. Phil. 3:3). He states that Abraham was "the father of all who believe without being circumcised" (Rom. 4:12). He does not have his associate Titus circumcised (Gal. 2:3). Yet, he has Timothy circumcised.

Likewise, today we do not compromise our conservative *principles* regarding proper constitutional government. But we sometimes have to alter our action (our *vote*) for the lesser of evils with a view to maintaining as many constitutional policies and practices as we can.

## Our Long-term Strategy

As I have been pointing out, we are in a socio-political struggle for the long run. Therefore, I have been urging that we act accordingly. Like it or not, in politics we cannot expect overnight success through one particular election or by means of a "perfect" candidate. To continually vote for the "perfect" candidate when we know he is going to lose does not help us build for the future, for by that we are ceding more victories to the overt liberals. Liberalism is messy. When its goo gets all over the place, it is very difficult to clean up the mess.

Why should we continually butt our heads against the wall each election cycle? It performs no useful service except for providing a steady drumbeat leading Christians in the march *away* from long-term influence. But what about those with less grandiose designs who hold that voting for the perfect Christian candidate will at least make "a statement"? More often than not they make the *wrong* statement: "Let's lose this one for Jesus." Their dismal poll numbers can make a statement, but not a very loud one. Sadly, conservative and moderate candidates can split the vote against the dangerous liberal candidate.

Recognizing the necessity of strategic compromise and incremental advance we should be willing to seek smaller political victories in the meantime. And rather than hoping against hope for the perfect presidential candidate to be elected, we will have to accept a tolerable candidate who functions like a finger in the dike effectively buying us more time — and keep us from throwing good money and our political hopes into a losing cause. Change tends to be generational rather than overnight.

We should not expect to change the nation in one fell swoop. Rather we should engage the more manageable work of changing a political party from within. Transforming a political party that is relatively close to several of our positions is easier than trying to change an entire nation that is literally "all over the map." Like it or not, American government is effectively a two-party system.

If worse comes to worse, we may eventually need to create a new political party from within the established lesser-of-evils party. But this would need to start out on a more local level and build toward higher offices and larger goals in the long run. For instance, today many Christians tend to put too much hope in the presidential election, hoping for the big prize. Turnouts in mid-term elections are generally around 20% small than in presidential elections. We should begin by working locally in small realms rather than trying to leap to the presidency.

Former Speaker of the House Tip O'Neill coined the phrase: "all politics is local." By that he meant that people tend to vote on matters of local interest and significance. This requires that politicians must recognize the needs of their constituencies. And since this is generally true, it also underscores the significance of learning about local needs by working in lower offices — as training for higher office.

Our nation used to be more acclimated to localism in its early days. Of course, slow transportation and limited communication had much to do with that. Today Christians need to take a greater (not *sole*) interest in local elections, such as mayoral, city and county councils, county administrators, sheriffs, and so forth. Once we have built success and gained experience in these more local areas, we can move on to state legislatures and governorships. And then to congressional and senatorial office, and on to the presidency. Secure foundations must be laid before a gold dome can be placed on the top.

## Conclusion

As conservative, evangelical Christians we are committed to principle at the very core of our being. The doctrinal convictions we hold regarding our holy faith serve as the very foundation for our lives — they are our most basic principles. And as servants of Christ we love and seek the right, just, and good. Consequently, it is difficult for us to compromise since our very lives are rooted in God-given principles.

We do not, of course, compromise our *principles* themselves. That would make us what we are not. But sometimes we must compromise our *methods*. In promoting Christian politics in a mixed and antagonistic environment such as we have in America, we must recognize the opposition we face. We must accept as a political principle that we will have to oppose the greater evil by sometimes voting for the lesser good.

In this chapter we have seen how our long term goal for victory must often involve a short term strategy which is painful but necessary. We must recognize the big picture and learn patience in seeking to bring it into proper focus. We saw how even theology and Scripture allow compromise in our methods in seeking the ultimate greater good. Voting the lesser of evils is necessary in a fallen world where all human action is tainted by evil.

CPSIA information can be obtained
at www.ICGtesting.com
Printed in the USA
FSHW021345161020
74800FS

9 780996 452588